Benefit-Cost Analyses of Social Regulation

Benefit-Cost Analyses of Social Regulation

Case Studies from the Council on Wage and Price Stability

Edited by
James C. Miller III
and Bruce Yandle

American Enterprise Institute for Public Policy Research
Washington, D.C.

Library of Congress Cataloging in Publication Data

Main entry under title:

Benefit-cost analyses of social regulation.

(AEI studies ;231)
1. Industry and state—United States—Cost effective-
ness. 2. Consumer protection—United States—Cost
effectiveness. 3. Environmental policy—United States
—Cost effectiveness. I. Miller III, James Clifford.
II. Yandle, Bruce. III. United States. Council on
Wage and Price Stability. IV. Series: American
Enterprise Institute for Public Policy Research. AEI
studies ;231
HC106.7.B46   338'.0973   79-876
ISBN 0-8447-3334-2

AEI Studies 231

Printed in the United States of America

CONTRIBUTORS

Co-Editors
James C. Miller III

Co-Director, Center for the Study of Government Regulation
American Enterprise Institute
Formerly Assistant Director for Government Operations and Research
Council on Wage and Price Stability

Bruce Yandle

Professor of Economics, Clemson University
Adjunct Scholar, American Enterprise Institute
Formerly Senior Economist
Council on Wage and Price Stability

Contributors
Robert L. Greene

Senior Economist, Environmental Protection Agency
Formerly Senior Economist
Council on Wage and Price Stability

Thomas D. Hopkins

Assistant Director for Government Programs and Regulation
Council on Wage and Price Stability
Formerly Assistant Professor of Economics, Bowdoin College

Milton Z. Kafoglis

Chairman and Professor of Economics
University of South Florida
Formerly Senior Economist
Council on Wage and Price Stability

Thomas M. Lenard

Senior Economist
Council on Wage and Price Stability
Formerly Assistant Professor of Economics
University of California at Davis

Dianne R. Levine

Senior Economist
Council on Wage and Price Stability
Formerly Assistant Professor of Economics and Statistics
California State University (Los Angeles)

Roger J. Mallet

Senior Economist, Department of Commerce
Formerly Senior Economist
Council on Wage and Price Stability

John F. Morrall III

Deputy Assistant Director of Government Programs and Regulation
Council on Wage and Price Stability
Formerly Assistant Professor of Economics
University of Florida

Gerald G. Threadgill

Budget Officer, United States Army
Formerly Senior Economist
Council on Wage and Price Stability
(on detail from U.S. Military Academy)

CONTENTS

PART TWO: PRODUCT SAFETY

PART THREE: ENERGY, THE ENVIRONMENT, AND INTERNATIONAL TRADE

List of Tables

List of Figures

1

Introduction

James C. Miller III and Bruce Yandle

Regulation of the U.S. economy to promote certain "social" goals like a cleaner environment, safer products, and a healthier workplace is not new. What is new is that during the 1970s the federal government's regulatory role has greatly expanded. Indeed, the rate of growth and all-pervading nature of regulation has raised another serious concern: the stubborn flames of inflation may have a new source of fuel. In fact, there is a growing awareness of a linkage between regulation and inflationary pressures. Because of this linkage, the benefits and costs of government regulatory actions must be considered with extreme care.

Consider the growth of the new regulation just during the decade. In 1970, the Environmental Protection Agency was established, followed by the Occupational Safety and Health Administration in 1971, and the Consumer Product Safety Commission in 1972. Between 1970 and 1977, the number of major federal social regulatory agencies rose from twelve to seventeen, total budgeted expenditures increased fivefold, and the number of pages printed annually in the *Federal Register* (the official publication carrying notices of federal rules and regulations) more than tripled (see Table 1–1). Of course, these indicators of cost merely begin to identify the full impact of regulation. Available estimates suggest that regulatory costs to the private sector may now exceed $100 billion annually.

This growing edge of federal regulation is not only large, it is different in character from that of the past. Instead of the more traditional economic regulation dealing with rates and services of specific firms and industries (for example, airlines, truckers, broadcasters, telephone and power companies), the new social regulation covers a broad range of industries and types of commercial activity. Moreover,

1

TABLE 1-1

INDEXES OF GROWTH IN FEDERAL REGULATION, 1970–1977

Year	Number of Major "Economic" Regulatory Agencies[a]	Number of Major "Social" Regulatory Agencies[b]	Expenditures of Major "Economic" Regulatory Agencies (millions of dollars)[c]	Expenditures of Major "Social" Regulatory Agencies (millions of dollars)[d]	Number of Pages in Federal Register	Number of Pages in Code of Federal Regulations
1970	8	12	166.1	1,449.3	20,036	54,105
1971	8	14	196.8	1,882.2	25,447	54,487
1972	8	14	246.3	2,247.5	28,924	61,035
1973	8	17	198.7	2,773.7	35,592	64,852
1974	9	17	304.3	3,860.1	42,422	69,270
1975	10	17	427.6	4,251.4	60,221	72,200
1976	10	17	489.8	5,028.3	57,072	73,149
1977	10	17	917.1[e]	7,318.3[e]	61,000[e]	75,000[e]
Percentage increase (1970–1977)	25	42	452	405	204	39

a Agencies included: Civil Aeronautics Board, Commodity Futures Trading Commission (1975–1977), Federal Communications Commission, Federal Energy Administration (1974–1977), Federal Maritime Commission, Federal Power Commission, Federal Trade Commission, International Trade Commission (1974–1977), Interstate Commerce Commission, Securities and Exchange Commission, and Tariff Commission (1970–1973).

b Agencies included: Agricultural Marketing Service (1972–1977), Atomic Energy Commission (1970–1974), Consumer and Marketing Service (1970–1971), Coast Guard, Consumer Product Safety Commission (1973–1977), Employment Standards Administration (1971–1977), Environmental Protection Agency, Equal Employment Opportunity Commission, Federal Aviation Administration, Federal Highway Administration, Federal Railroad Administration, Food and Drug Administration, Mining Enforcement and Safety Administration (1973–1977), National Highway Traffic Safety Administration, National Labor Relations Board, National Transportation Safety Board (1971–1977), Nuclear Regulatory Commission (1975–1977), Occupational Safety and Health Administration (1973–1977), Occupational Safety and Health Review Commission (1971–1977), and Workplace Standards Administration.

c Taken from The Budget of the United States, 1972–1977.

d Taken from The Budget of the United States, 1972–1977. Total expenditures of all agencies listed in footnote b above, except only health- and safety-related expenditures for the following agencies: Atomic Energy Commission (1970–1974; "regulatory activities"), Coast Guard ("operating expenses": merchant marine safety and marine law enforcement/marine environmental protection), Federal Aviation Administration ("operations": flight standards program, medical standards program; "facilities": engineering and development; and "safety regulation"), Federal Highway Administration ("motor carrier and highway safety"), and Federal Railroad Administration ("safety regulation" ("Bureau of Railroad Safety").

e Estimated.

SOURCE: For 1970–1975, see William Lilley III and James C. Miller III, "The New Social Regulation," The Public Interest (Spring 1977), p. 50 (AEI Reprint no. 66); for 1976–1977, up-date provided by Keith McGowan.

3

it is highly specific in terms of its requirements. For example, regulations dictate the contents of labels attached to consumer products, prescribe in minute detail a multitude of work practices, mandate specific processes for the treatment of industrial wastes, and establish uniform designs for products as simple as book matches or as complex as automobiles.

If one theme underlies the statutory approach to social regulation, it is the desire for *perfection*—for a world without risk. While everyone dreams of Utopia, at some point society is forced to ask, "Is such perfection in fact feasible?" And if so, "Is a step in that direction worth the cost?" In short, social problems and their solutions take on an economic dimension. The old problems of scarcity and necessary trade-offs cannot be avoided.

Benefit-Cost Analysis

Economists have developed a technique for evaluating programs that involve scarcity and trade-offs. It is called "benefit-cost analysis." Although much maligned by its detractors, benefit-cost analysis can be most useful to a policy maker. Basically, all it entails is weighing the benefits and costs of a proposal before action is taken. At one extreme, the analysis might be no more quantitative than the policy maker's concluding that he or she "feels" the benefits of an action outweigh the costs (or the other way around). At the other extreme are the highly sophisticated estimates of benefits and costs usually conjured up at the mention of the term "benefit-cost analysis."

Without question, estimating benefits and costs is often difficult, especially in the areas of social regulation, where the benefits may be in terms of lives saved or pain and suffering avoided. Some say this means putting a value on human pain, suffering, and death, which is not only ludicrous, but downright immoral. If anything, we would argue, the reverse is true. Since resources are limited, we cannot avoid the need to identify—and, in some way, to estimate—benefits and costs. The more compassion we have for our fellow human beings, the more important this becomes. For benefit-cost analysis is merely a shorthand summary expression of who would benefit by how much from a proposed policy change, and who would be forced to sacrifice, at what cost. Indeed, benefit-cost analysis can point the way toward increasing the degree of perfection by identifying ways to minimize costs. Whether or not benefit-cost studies are used, however, *every* policy action reveals that, in the mind of the decision maker(s), benefits do exceed costs and that the distribution of benefits and costs is socially desirable. Thus, all policy decisions—whether to adopt a new initiative, to modify it, or to accept the status quo—reveal an implicit benefit-cost analysis.

Benefit-cost analysis really has two dimensions. The first is that of aiding the decision maker in deciding whether a given proposal should or should not be adopted. That is, "Do the benefits (somehow measured) exceed the costs (also somehow measured)?" In practice, this may simply be a listing of the measurable benefits on one side of the ledger and the measurable costs on the other, and then noting the various subjective benefits and costs to be weighed in the balance. The second dimension of benefit-cost analysis has to do with analyzing alternatives. That is, are there alternative ways of securing the same social regulatory objective that impose lower costs on society, or at least distribute the costs differently? Or, for a given cost, are there alternatives that would come closer to the goal of perfection, or at least result in a different distribution of the benefits? This use of benefit-cost analysis to evaluate alternatives is sometimes called "cost-effectiveness analysis." Basically, it is nothing more than an application of the efficiency axiom: maximize production for a given total cost; or minimize total cost for a given level of production.

The Council on Wage and Price Stability

Benefit-cost analysis has been a part of the economist's tool kit for at least a decade and was applied to many government programs as part of the "planning-programming-budgeting" (PPB) review efforts promulgated by the federal Bureau of the Budget during the 1960s. But, because PPB and its successor program, "management by objectives" (MBO), were phased out, the federal government's mushrooming social regulatory activities during the early 1970s were not subjected to benefit-cost analysis in any systematic way. This was changed, however, when in 1974 Congress created the Council on Wage and Price Stability and President Ford initiated the Inflation Impact Statement program.

On August 20, 1974, the Council on Wage and Price Stability was established to monitor activities of the private sector of the economy that might add to the rate of inflation. In addition, the council was directed to "review the activities and programs of the Federal government to discover whether they have any inflationary impact." From the very beginning, the council interpreted this mandate as requiring benefit-cost analyses of important regulatory actions. Thus, a microeconomic tool joined a macro battle.

The council argued that a narrow focus on the impact of federal regulations on conventional price indexes such as the consumer price index (CPI) would not be particularly helpful since the impact on a gross statistic such as the CPI of even the most costly regulation would be minimal and difficult to determine with any precision, and many benefits and costs of regulatory activity would not show up in the price indexes or would appear in contradictory ways.[1] Instead, the council adopted the view that the major policy instruments determining the rate of inflation were fiscal and monetary policy, but that —whatever fiscal and monetary policies were chosen—any policy action that increased the aggregate supply of goods and services would lower the rate of inflation and vice versa. This meant that a government regulation which generated benefits (that is, the addition to aggregate supply) greater than costs (the subtraction from aggregate supply) was in a real sense anti-inflationary. On the other hand, a regulatory initiative generating costs in excess of benefits would have to be labeled inflationary. Also, any regulation that was not cost-effective was also inflationary, even though benefits might exceed costs. This basic approach was also adopted by the council when it was given a major role in administering the Inflation Impact Statement program. Under the program, for their major proposed regulations, agencies were required to estimate and analyze the benefits of the proposal, its costs, and the benefits and costs of alternative approaches.

Thus, because of a legislative mandate and the Inflation Impact Statement program, virtually all regulatory agencies came under the purview of the council, where a small group of economists reviewed newly proposed regulations and their supporting documents. The product of this staff of economists took several forms. In most cases, the council's views were expressed through official written comments or "filings," which became a part of the formal record in regulatory proceedings. At other times, the views of the staff were expressed in public testimony at the agency. In still other instances, detailed analyses were provided to agencies as a part of an "internal review" procedure. And in yet other cases, the staff initiated studies of significant regulatory issues not related to any official regulatory proceeding. In many instances, proposed regulations were accompanied

---

[1] Take, for example, a regulation to require a firm to reduce the amount of effluent it discharges into a river. A price index would reflect benefits in the form of lower costs of processing downstream river water into drinking water (the effect of which would be to lower the price index), but benefits in terms of having the river cleaner for purposes of fishing, swimming, or just being near would show up in terms of higher land rents (raising the index).

by Inflationary Impact Statements, and these were often relied upon by the council's staff in developing its analysis of the potential inflationary impact of the regulatory proposal.

Contents of the Volume

This volume contains case studies that are taken directly from the work of economists on the council's staff. The topics represented are almost as diverse as the contents of the *Federal Register*. Even so, we have placed them into broad categories that organize the book into three distinct parts: (1) consumer and worker health, (2) product safety, and (3) energy, the environment, and international trade.[2] Each case study is a complete and independent unit that can be turned to, read, and discussed without having read those that came before. A short introduction at the beginning of each case gives some background to the issue analyzed. Also, in editing the cases, we have attempted to retain the original tone and character of the analysts' report.

It should be noted that the presentations summarized here were usually part of a long, and sometimes arduous, regulatory process. In some cases, the proceedings have been completed and final regulatory action has been taken. In others, the deliberations continue. At the end of each selection, we have inserted a brief note to bring the reader up to date.

Part One of the volume contains cases on consumer and worker health. An analysis by Ms. Dianne Levine considers proposed regulations for labeling blood according to the type of supplier. The issue relates to consumer information and the relative benefits and costs of differentiating purchased blood from that taken from volunteers. A second analysis by Ms. Levine treats the problem of worker exposure to inorganic arsenic. The issue here is a proposal by the Occupational Safety and Health Administration (OSHA) to reduce the maximum allowable exposure level far below that which would be required for reasons of toxicity. A third case, an OSHA proposal addressed by Dr. John Morrall, deals with the question of how far to reduce the maximum allowable noise level experienced by industrial workers. Both OSHA analyses illustrate the ubiquitous phenomenon mentioned earlier: that, as we strive to achieve perfection, the costs rise markedly whereas the additional benefits tend to decline.

---

[2] Technically, international trade is an instance of conventional economic regulation, not social regulation. We consider, however, that the merits of including it in the volume outweigh presumed concerns for consistency. Such is our benefit-cost analysis.

In Part Two, on product safety, Dr. Thomas Lenard analyzes a proposal by the Consumer Product Safety Commission (CPSC) that would require manufacturers of lawn mowers to install certain safety devices. Dr. Milton Kafoglis analyzes another CPSC proposal—to issue standards for the production of ordinary matchbooks. These two cases illustrate a fairly common aspect of regulatory proposals— that is, certain components of the proposed standards appear cost-effective, while others do not. In these cases, clear questions are raised about the "reasonableness" of the requirements that dead-man switches be installed on the lawn mowers and that latches be installed on matchbooks.

The selection by Dr. Thomas Hopkins and Mr. Gerald Thread-gill addresses another safety issue—an early proposal by the National Highway Traffic Safety Administration to require passive restraints in automobiles (for example, air bags). This is a particularly interesting case, for it suggests that use by auto passengers of the safety devices at hand (seat belts) could eliminate the need for much more costly passive restraint systems.

In Part Three, on energy, the environment, and international trade, Dr. Milton Kafoglis and Dr. Robert Greene address a proposal by the Federal Energy Administration (now a part of the Department of Energy) to require manufacturers of appliances to improve the overall "energy efficiency" of their products in steps over the coming years. This is basically a cost-effectiveness issue. How should standards be set so as to minimize the cost to society of meeting a given objective (which in this case is a reduction in energy consumption by appliances)?

Three environmental regulatory issues are treated next. Mr. Roger Mallet analyzes a proposal by the Environmental Protection Agency (EPA) to place a limit on the air emissions of motorcycles, and Dr. Robert Greene analyzes an EPA proposal to require manufacturers of iron and steel to reduce effluents discharged into the nation's waterways. In both cases, the analysts raise questions about the overall severity of the standards and point to modifications that would lower the cost of achieving the regulatory goal. Then, Dr. John Morrall analyzes proposals by the EPA and the Federal Aviation Administration to reduce noise exposure around airports by requiring that old aircraft be "retrofitted" or that the airlines acquire new, quieter aircraft. Dr. Morrall concludes that a tax-incentive approach to reducing such noise exposure would be far superior to the standards approach favored by the government agencies.

The final selection, by Dr. Thomas Lenard, deals with a proposal before the International Trade Commission to grant relief to the U.S. sugar industry because of rising sugar imports. In concise fashion, Dr. Lenard analyzes the costs (and who bears them) and the benefits (and who receives them) of the major alternatives: quotas, tariffs, and adjustment assistance. This analysis is especially timely because of increasing calls for protection of U.S. industry.

Although these analyses were primarily produced by those listed as the authors, in every instance the final product reflected inputs from attorneys as well as economists. In fact, these works represent a rather significant precedent since, with one exception,[3] all the case studies were taken from formal filings (before regulatory agencies) that were signed by both attorneys and economists. Although the attorneys' work was primarily that of identifying for the agency the council's authority to intervene and why the recommendations of the council were pertinent to the decision, the economists' analyses were often improved significantly by the attorneys' efforts. Thus, all of the authors join us in acknowledging the legal expertise contributed by other officials at the council. These included Peter Lowry, Paul McAuliffe, Roy Nierenberg, and Vaughn Williams. The work of public affairs officer Morris Feibusch and research assistants Stephen Niemczyk and Debra Paxson is also gratefully acknowledged.

Finally, the authors want to acknowledge the contributions of other council officials, including Michael Moskow and William Lilley, who took final responsibility for these efforts, and Albert Rees and George Eads, who were responsible for initiating the program of regulatory analysis.[4]

Concluding Remarks

What conclusions can we draw about federal regulation from these case studies? There are several. One is that legislation often constrains the extent to which benefit-cost analysis is taken into consideration when promulgating regulations. In some cases, that

---

[3] Dr. Morrall's analysis of the airport noise issue was a study initiated by the council and was submitted as an attachment to congressional testimony.

[4] Dr. Albert Rees was director of the council from its inception until 1975, when he returned to Princeton University. Dr. George Eads was the assistant director in charge of government programs from the council's inception until he took over as acting director from Dr. Rees and became executive director of the National Commission on Supplies and Shortages a few months later. Dr. Michael Moskow became director in September 1975, leaving in the spring of 1976 to become under secretary of labor. At that time, Dr. William Lilley, who had served as the council's deputy director under Dr. Moskow, became acting director.

interpretation is made because of somewhat ambiguous wording in the legislation. For example, OSHA is required to reduce worker exposure to unhealthful substances wherever "technically feasible," and the agency has tended to interpret this as meaning without regard to benefits and costs. A second lesson is that agencies develop considerable momentum and tend to reflect the views of the constituents that supported their formation. Thus, for example, proposals by the Consumer Product Safety Commission are typically tough on the side of consumers, and OSHA proposals are equally tough on the side of organized labor. A third lesson is that economic analysis can be very useful in appraising the performance of regulatory agencies. Since agencies do not typically overlap in their regulatory responsibilities, there is not the spur of competition that exists in the private sector. That is, inefficient agencies are not weeded out and supplanted by more efficient agencies. For this reason, it is extremely important that the performance of agencies be monitored closely, and benefit-cost analysis is an appropriate tool for this purpose.

Has benefit-cost analysis of the type contained in this volume had a significant impact on the regulatory process? We find no simple answers. We do, however, find that, as more and more critical attention is directed toward regulatory phenomena, agency personnel express greater interest in acquiring the skills of economic analysis and in using such analysis in their decision-making process. It is our hope that this publication will be helpful in that learning process.

PART ONE

Consumer and Worker Health

2

Labeling Donated Blood

Dianne R. Levine

In 1971, the Department of Health, Education and Welfare (HEW) took the first steps toward developing a National Blood Policy. To a large extent, that initiative resulted from a concern that an adequate supply of blood be provided for transfusion purposes and yet that the incidence of post-transfusion hepatitis be minimized. While blood is supplied through both voluntary and commercial operations, the incidence of hepatitis in the United States has been higher with purchased blood. For this reason, the U.S. Blood Policy, announced in 1973, espoused the goal of creating an all-volunteer blood supply system. This analysis is based on a proposed HEW regulation to label blood as volunteer or commercial. The issue is so important that it was the subject of a conference sponsored by the American Enterprise Institute in June 1976.[1]

The Food and Drug Administration (FDA) has proposed regulations that would require that whole blood and red blood cells bear a statement distinguishing blood from volunteer donors and blood from paid donors, and a warning that blood collected from paid donors is associated with a higher risk of transmitting hepatitis.[2] Because this proposal could have a significant impact both on the availability of blood and on inflation, it should be closely evaluated.

The premise on which the proposed regulations rest is not ques-

---

This chapter is edited from "Whole Blood and Red Blood Cells," Comments of the Council on Wage and Price Stability before the Food and Drug Administration, Docket No. 75N-0316, January 13, 1976.

[1] See David B. Johnson, ed., *Blood Policy: Issues and Alternatives* (Washington, D.C.: American Enterprise Institute, 1977).

[2] 40 Fed. Reg. 53040 (November 1975).

tioned—that is, the incidence of post-transfusion hepatitis associated with blood from paid donors (that is, from commercial blood banks) is substantially higher than the incidence associated with other blood. Such information should certainly be made available to patients, their relatives, and their physicians. In fact, the proposed regulations would increase the amount of information available to consumers at relatively little cost.[3]

Certain minor changes should, however, be made in the final regulations to ensure that the information to be placed on the label is both accurate and informative. Moreover, the proposed regulations should be modified so as to provide for review and revision within five years of the date of promulgation. At that time, the FDA could determine whether changes in the technology of blood testing had rendered the premise on which the proposed regulations are based incorrect and whether the regulations have had any adverse effects on the market for blood.

Nature of the Problem

At the present time, 10 to 15 percent of the domestic blood supply originates in commercial blood banks where donors are paid cash directly and immediately. This blood is generally associated with an incidence of post-transfusion hepatitis that is between three and ten times the incidence associated with blood from volunteer donors. The usual reason given for this fact is as follows.

The people who sell blood for cash tend to be poor, drug addicts, or derelicts who feel an immediate need of the $5 to $30 that is offered for a pint of blood. These people are often sick, undernourished, and carriers of hepatitis as well as other diseases. This logic states that the cash these people will be given for their blood acts as an overwhelming incentive for them to lie about their physical condition, to donate too frequently, and, most important, to conceal bouts of hepatitis they may have experienced. Existing methods of testing blood are not sufficiently sensitive to detect hepatitis infection. Thus, infected blood cannot be avoided completely without the cooperation of the donor—that is, the donor must give accurate information. Volunteer donors—or those donors who contribute blood at community blood banks, hospitals, and Red Cross centers—are pre-

---

[3] Current labeling practices and procedures make it possible for all units of blood to be traced back to the original donor. The additional cost of labeling units of blood as either volunteer or commercial, at point of collection, would be minimal.

sumably motivated by humanitarian feelings and are more likely to disclose accurate facts about their own health status even though this might lead to refusal of their blood.

This reasoning has led to the proposed regulations. But one important effect of these regulations (if promulgated) might be to eliminate commercial donors nationwide. A similar 1973 law in the state of Illinois has thus far reduced the number of units of purchased blood infused by 35.2 percent, despite a 15 percent increase in the total number of transfusions between fiscal year 1974 and fiscal year 1975.[4] The Illinois law also requires physicians to state on their patients' charts their reasons for using the riskier blood.

An Alternative View

The normal line of reasoning, however, is open to question. It is possible that the regulations, as proposed, would have deleterious effects on the cost of blood. Moreover, the proposed regulations might indirectly and subtly lead to the implementation of certain aspects of the National Blood Policy that should be examined.[5]

First, the distinction between paid donor and volunteer donor, as it pertains to the issue here, is more apparent than real. The notion that all donors who give blood at Red Cross centers, hospitals, and community blood banks are giving for humanitarian and altruistic reasons is naive and grossly inaccurate. It is estimated that less than 10 percent of all blood used in the United States has been altruistically given.[6] The rest of the so-called volunteer donations have been given by persons who are replacing blood used by their friends or relatives (thereby helping them avoid fees for blood used) or who are insuring against their families' possible blood requirements in the future. Only a very narrow definition of paid donor would omit these donors. These people also have a great incentive to conceal their experiences with hepatitis. Although the incidence of the disease is lower in this (wealthier) portion of the population, the incentives to conceal pertinent health information are just as real as they are in the case of commercial donors.

---

[4] 40 Fed. Reg. 53040 (November 1975).

[5] The National Blood Policy, which espouses the goal of creating an all-volunteer blood system, was announced in the *Federal Register* of July 10, 1973.

[6] See Marc A. Franklin, "Tort Liability for Hepatitis: An Analysis and a Proposal," *Stanford Law Review*, vol. 24 (1972), p. 439, which uses the definition from Richard M. Titmuss, *The Gift Relationship: From Human Blood to Social Policy* (New York: Pantheon, 1971).

Second, not all purchased blood is associated with a high risk of hepatitis. The Mayo Clinic in Minnesota and the University of Iowa Hospital have been largely dependent on commercial sources for blood, yet their incidence of post-transfusion hepatitis has been low. Sweden pays all its blood donors, yet the incidence of post-transfusion hepatitis there is lower than it is in the United States. Thus, it would be misleading to patients and physicians to require a label on all blood from paid donors stating that the blood carries a high risk of transmitting hepatitis. A particular commercial source might be able to show that in the past its blood has been associated with an incidence of hepatitis that is no higher than that of blood from volunteer donors.

Third, blood currently collected is linked to about 17,000 cases of overt post-transfusion hepatitis each year and some 850 deaths. The average cost of these cases is about $23,225, excluding pain and suffering.[7] It is estimated that about 85,000 subclinical cases of this disease also occur as a result of transfusions.[8] Although somewhere between 25 and 45 percent of these cases were probably linked to commercial blood, between 55 and 75 percent of the cases are attributable to voluntarily donated blood. Thus, although the probability of contracting hepatitis is greater with a unit of commercial blood, in terms of total cases volunteer blood appears to be the main cause.

Fourth, the National Blood Policy strongly "support[s] efforts to bring into being an all-voluntary blood donation system and to eliminate commercialism in the acquisition of whole blood and blood components for transfusion purposes."[9] It may be appropriate for a national policy statement to appeal to humanitarian motives and other lofty ideals, but it is questionable whether sole reliance upon such motives would be sufficient to obtain enough quality blood of the type needed. Thus far, the United States has had to rely on commercial blood banks to supply up to 15 percent of the blood used, even though 25 percent of all blood currently collected is discarded because it becomes outdated.[10]

---

[7] Reuben Kessel, *Journal of Law and Economics*, October 1974, pp. 268–69. Data were obtained from the 1973 Conference on the National Blood Policy and from Richard Thaler and Sherwin Rosen, *Estimating the Value of Saving a Life: Evidence from the Labor Market*, no. 36 (New York: National Bureau of Economic Research, Conference on Research in Income and Wealth, December 1, 1973).

[8] 39 Fed. Reg. 32703 (1974).

[9] Ibid., p. 32702.

[10] The major reason is that peak times for donation do not coincide with peaks in use.

The U.S. public policies toward blood would be improved sub-stantially if blood were recognized as a product that is not very different from other consumer goods. No blood is "free" even if it is given voluntarily or altruistically. The cost of obtaining a unit of blood from an unpaid donor is not zero even when preparation and processing costs are excluded. Resources expended to solicit this blood, time of the volunteer donor, time of the volunteer worker, the side effects of giving blood, and the increased risk of disease that the donor bears are all very real costs of blood. The main difference in treatment of the costs of purchased blood and of volunteered blood is that in the former case the donor has been compensated in cash by the collection agency, whereas in the latter case satisfaction or avoidance of group pressure has served as compensation to the donor. The actual blood collected differs because of the different strata of society that are appealed to by the differing forms of compensation.

The quality of the blood collected—that is, its average disease-bearing characteristics—varies considerably for different reasons. In general, the public is largely unaware of the risks and the quality of transfused blood. Physicians and hospitals do not have enough in-centive to search for quality blood. The liability laws of various states have contributed to the acceptance and use of poor quality blood. Another contributing factor has been the refusal of public policy makers to accept prices that differ according to the quality of blood and that reflect actual costs of procurement.

Competition among suppliers, both commercial and nonprofit, together with basic regulations of quality and testing procedures, should be encouraged. Organizations could then solicit donors in any lawful manner. They would assure quality by extensive and expensive testing or by careful selection of donors who are monitored for disease and are encouraged to donate repeatedly. These people could be paid in order to make it worthwhile to give at the most needed times. Cases in which a recipient reacts to a donor's blood (particularly, cases of post-transfusion hepatitis) would be traced back to the donor and that donor would be eliminated from the pool of blood donors. The collection agencies would be liable for product safety and quality just as any other producer is liable for defects in his product.

The competitive market for blood need not exclude blood that is associated with a higher risk of hepatitis. Such blood would be safe for use in treating patients, such as many hemophiliacs, who have already had serum hepatitis and who are therefore immune to the disease. These users would be encouraged to use such blood by its lower price.

Contrary to what is implied by the National Blood Policy, increased commercialism may be the most appropriate way to alleviate the inefficiencies, shortages, and poor quality of product that currently pervade blood programs in the United States. Before the FDA seriously contemplates the adoption of regulations that would further the National Blood Policy, the agency should make a careful study of these points.

Conclusion

The proposed regulations should be approved subject to the following modifications:

- The label should indicate clearly and quantitatively the risk of hepatitis from volunteer blood.

- The label should indicate clearly and quantitatively the risk of hepatitis from commercial blood (thus showing the difference in risk).

- Suppliers of commercial blood that can demonstrate better records than the average for commercial blood should be allowed to include this information prominently on their labels.

Moreover, one aspect of the National Blood Policy—namely, the goal of eliminating all commercial blood—should be reevaluated. It is difficult to see how the elimination of *any* class of blood would be beneficial to consumers. Surely, there must be instances in which marginally inferior blood is preferable to no blood at all. In fact, encouraging *more* commercialism in blood delivery—under appropriate safeguards—may be the most appropriate way of assuring adequate supplies of quality blood at low prices. In any event, this possibility should be reviewed in detail before any substantial parts of the National Blood Policy are implemented.

On January 13, 1978, the Food and Drug Administration issued its final regulations requiring blood and blood components intended for transfusion to be labeled either "paid donor" or "volunteer donor."[11] *A paid donor was defined as a person who receives monetary payment for a blood donation, and a volunteer donor does not receive*

---

[11] 43 Fed. Reg. 2142 (1978).

such payment. The final labeling rule omitted the warning statement, originally proposed, concerning the increased risks of hepatitis from blood collected from paid donors. This omission was an acknowledgment that many blood banks (in hospitals and research centers particularly) use paid donor blood yet have lower rates of hepatitis among their patients than other all-volunteer blood banks. The final notice of rule making did reiterate support for an all-volunteer donor system, but stress was placed on the need for better monitoring of donors and improved blood testing.

3

Exposure to Inorganic Arsenic in the Workplace

Dianne R. Levine

The Occupational Safety and Health Act of 1970 is a prime example of legislation that spawned an extensive array of social regulations. Since its creation by the act, the Occupational Safety and Health Administration (OSHA) has sought to accomplish its legislated mandate —the assurance of a safe workplace for all Americans—by issuing detailed engineering standards. Quite often, alternative ways to reduce accidents and increase life expectancy have been called to the attention of OSHA. The agency, however, has seldom steered away from engineering standards, even when cost-effectiveness arguments were quite persuasive. This analysis of a proposed arsenic standard illustrates an application of benefit-cost analysis to the problem of maximizing the number of lives saved, given a resource constraint.

On January 21, 1975, OSHA proposed a revised standard for exposure to inorganic arsenic in the workplace.[1] The proposal would require smelters, herbicide producers, and others to install engineering controls to reduce the maximum exposure level for workers from the present 0.5 milligrams of arsenic per cubic meter of air to 0.004 milligrams.

More specifically, the proposed standard sets a maximum concentration of 0.004 milligrams of arsenic per cubic meter of air (0.004 mg As/m^3) averaged over an eight-hour period. In addition, a ceiling limit of 0.01 milligrams is proposed for any fifteen-minute

---

This chapter is edited from "Exposure to Inorganic Arsenic Proposed Standard," Statement on Behalf of the Council on Wage and Price Stability before the Occupational Safety and Health Administration, Docket No. OSH-37, September 14, 1976.

[1] 40 Fed. Reg. 3392 (January 21, 1975).

period. The proposed standard represents a 125-fold reduction in the permissible level of worker exposure. The proposal would require that employers "immediately institute feasible engineering controls to reduce employee exposure to inorganic arsenic to at or below 0.004 mg As/m³."[2] In those plants where engineering controls "will not reduce exposure to the permissible level, they must nonetheless be implemented to reduce exposures to the lowest practical level, and be supplemented by the use of work practice controls or respirators to provide necessary protection."[3]

The proposed standard sets an "action level" of 0.002 milligrams per cubic meter of air averaged over an eight-hour period. "The purpose of the action level is to set a level at which airborne inorganic arsenic can be practicably detected by the employer, and above which precautionary measures such as medical surveillance and monitoring are warranted."[4] Also included in the proposed standard are a number of general provisions dealing with matters such as regulated areas, labeling of arsenic containers, exposure measurement, employee training, extensive record keeping, and provision of change houses, respirators, protective clothing, and protective equipment.

This study evaluates OSHA's economic analysis of the proposed standard, which was released on June 24, 1976.[5] The study concludes that the analysis makes a reasonable attempt to estimate costs but is lacking in its estimates of benefits and in its discussion of alternatives. Moreover, in view of the certain large costs associated with going forward with engineering controls and the substantial questions remaining about benefits, this study urges that, if the standard is tightened, engineering controls not be specified at this time.

Analysis of Costs

OSHA's analysis estimates that the cost of compliance with the proposed standard would amount to approximately $273 million in initial capital costs and approximately $56 million additional in annual operating and maintenance costs. If, according to the analysis, the capital costs were spread out over eight years at a 12 percent interest rate, the total annual costs would be roughly $111 million. OSHA also estimates that between 350 and 380 additional workers would

---

[2] Ibid., p. 3397.

[3] Ibid.

[4] Ibid., p. 3396.

[5] Arthur Young and Company, *Inflationary Impact Statement: Inorganic Arsenic*, prepared for the Occupational Safety and Health Administration, April 28, 1976.

be required to maintain current levels of output. Nationwide, employment would be expected to decline by 3,000 to 3,700 workers because of a reduction in the sales of products of industries affected by this standard.[6]

Unfortunately, the OSHA cost estimates were obtained from only a limited number of plants. OSHA's report states: "In some instances whole industries were not represented in available data. . . . Cost estimates for the great majority of firms affected were either completely unavailable or fragmentary."[7] As a matter of fact, detailed cost estimates were obtained only for the zinc, lead, and copper smelting industries.[8] Other industries, however, would be affected by the proposed regulation, and here costs are difficult to obtain. Such costs were estimated by extrapolation of costs for a number of plants of different sizes when data for one plant in the industry were available or by analogy based primarily upon production levels and process similarities.

Costs to the wood-preserving industry present a particular problem for cost estimation. This industry consists of two large firms and a few hundred small, family-operated firms in which processes are less likely to be automated. In these smaller firms, compliance would be more costly to achieve because relatively massive changes in plant and equipment would probably be required. Automation of the process is usually necessary before the worker can be removed from the areas of intense arsenic exposure. Since the estimated initial costs of compliance for this industry are $82 million (out of total initial compliance costs of $270 million), small errors in cost estimation can be significant.

The proposed standard could significantly affect competition in the wood-preserving industry because compliance would be a much

---

[6] This includes not only the decrease in the quantity of arsenic demanded but also the decrease in the quantity of other commodities demanded in which arsenic is used as an input (for example, preserved wood and copper).

[7] Arthur Young and Company, *Inflationary Impact Statement*, pp. V–1 and V–2.

[8] The first study, performed for OSHA by D.B. Associates (under the direction of Arthur Young and Company), discusses three primary copper smelters: ASARCO's plants in Tacoma, Washington, and Hayden, Arizona; and Anaconda's plant. See D.B. Associates, *The Proposed Arsenic Standard: Feasibility and Estimated Costs of Compliance for Three U.S. Copper Smelters*, prepared for the Occupational Safety and Health Administration, March 25, 1976. The other study, performed for ASARCO by Industrial Health Engineering Associates, Inc., discusses ASARCO's plants in Tacoma, Washington; Globe, Arizona (metallic arsenic); Hayden, Arizona; El Paso, Texas; East Helena, Montana (zinc); and Glover, Missouri (lead). See Industrial Health Engineering Associates, *Feasibility and Cost Study to Achieve Various Concentrations of Arsenic Workroom Air at ASARCO Operations*, prepared for ASARCO, Inc., March 1975.

more onerous burden on the smaller firms than on the two large companies that dominate the industry. Moreover, despite the imprecise and admittedly speculative nature of some of the data, no *ranges* of cost have been provided.

Analysis of Benefits

OSHA's economic analysis discusses the information that is essential to any calculation of the value of reduced illness and deaths attributable to the proposed regulation: the size of the population at risk, the excess mortality and morbidity experienced by this population, and a monetary measure of life and health. Yet, despite apparently understanding the correct methodology for calculating benefits, OSHA makes no attempt to employ it. The analysis rests the case for adopting the proposed standard solely on the basis of summaries of five epidemiological studies of very small populations placed at risk by arsenic exposure levels that are substantially in excess of the current 0.5 milligram standard.[9]

The epidemiological studies cited deduce a significant association between worker exposure to arsenic and mortality from respiratory cancer. Although this study is not the work of a technical expert in the area of epidemiology, a few remarks can be ventured. First, the studies appear to have been properly conducted with suitable controls. Generally, in the more recent studies, the number of deaths caused primarily by respiratory cancer was compared with the expected number of deaths from that cause for each age group. The proportionate mortality experience from respiratory cancer for the group exposed to arsenic was compared with that for the general population. A causal relationship between arsenic and cancer could not be deduced, particularly because workers who were exposed to arsenic were also exposed to other toxic substances such as lead and sulfur dioxide. Nevertheless, OSHA and the National Institute for Occupational Safety and Health (NIOSH) concluded from these studies that inorganic arsenic is likely to be a carcinogen. This conclusion will not be contested here. It should be noted, however, that the apparent carcinogenic effect of arsenic (deduced by OSHA and NIOSH) was observed among populations that had been exposed to arsenic at concentrations of 1.0 to 5.0 milligrams or more of arsenic per cubic meter of air as opposed to the 0.5 standard now in effect or the proposed 0.004 standard. The workers who were included in those studies had been working with arsenic during the first half of the

---

[9] Arthur Young and Company, *Inflationary Impact Statement*, p. III–8.

century, prior to most attempts to control arsenic in the workplace and prior to any real knowledge about its possible carcinogenicity.

On the basis of the evidence in the five studies, the authors of OSHA's analysis conclude that the incidence rate of respiratory cancer among the arsenic-exposed population is likely to range from two to ten times that of the general (nonexposed) population. They steadfastly refrain, however, from using these proportionate mortality and incidence rates to arrive at estimates of excess deaths that could be attributed to arsenic exposure. It is true that the exact calculation of the benefits is limited by data deficiencies in the area of the relationship between dose and response and the relationship between duration and level of human exposure to inorganic arsenic and subsequent health effects. Nevertheless, various assumptions about these relationships, representing differing theories of cancer causation, could be made. This would provide a range of estimates of the benefits that could be obtained from promulgating the standard.

Applying alternative hypotheses about the relationship between dose and response and alternative hypotheses about the way duration and level of dose interact to affect health yields ranges of incidence of respiratory cancer for each level of exposure. These incidences can then be applied to the population at risk to obtain the range of expected excess deaths at each exposure level.[10]

Figure 3–1 illustrates graphically how alternative hypotheses about the dose and response relationship could be used to derive expected incidences of respiratory cancer among workers who would be exposed to lower levels of arsenic than those found in the cited studies. As a rough maximum estimate of excess deaths or benefits of the proposed standard, the conclusion that the incidence of respiratory cancer among the arsenic-exposed population is likely to range from two to ten times that of the general (nonexposed) population has been used. According to OSHA's analysis, the number of people currently exposed to arsenic levels in excess of the proposed standard is approximately 7,400 each year, after allowance has been made for the turnover rate. The incidence of respiratory cancer among males age thirty and older is about 160 cases per 100,000 in the general population. This suggests that the crude (unadjusted for age or sex) annual incidence of respiratory cancer for the exposed population is between 320 and 1,600 per 100,000. Under these assumptions, the number of excess cases of respiratory cancer resulting from arsenic exposure would be between 12 and 106 annually.

---

[10] Since respiratory cancer is fatal in more than 95 percent of the cases, the mortality rate can be approximated from the incidence with little loss in accuracy.

FIGURE 3–1

ALTERNATIVE HYPOTHESES CONCERNING DOSE-RESPONSE RELATIONSHIP

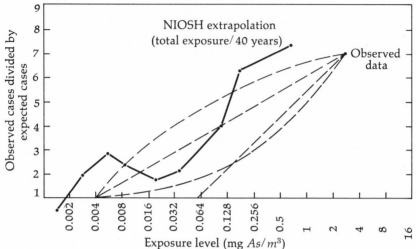

These figures grossly overestimate the benefits from the proposed standards. First, as mentioned above, the studies on which the estimates of excess mortality are based analyzed populations experiencing exposure levels ranging from two to ten times the present (0.5) standard. Second, not all the estimated 7,400 workers at risk are exposed to arsenic at the 0.5 standard level.[11] Third, since there is evidence that mortality is directly related to exposure level, the actual reductions in mortality that would accrue from the proposed standard would likely be significantly less than the range of 12 to 106 workers given above.

Fourth, the studies cited by OSHA use proportional mortality rates converted into lifetime incidences, whereas the incidence used above is an annual rate. Lifetime incidences of respiratory cancer are substantially less than the number of years an average person lives past the age of thirty, times the annual incidence for the general population over age thirty. In other words, the probability of a person's contracting respiratory cancer is not the sum of the probabilities of his contracting the disease each year of his life. This means that, if the turnover rate among arsenic-exposed workers is relatively low, a

---

[11] For example, OSHA's analysis notes that only 1,600 to 1,800 of those workers are exposed to levels beyond 0.1, one-fifth of the present standard; see Arthur Young and Company, *Inflation Impact Statement*, p. III–3.

large proportion of the exposed population consists of the same people for many years. The use of two to ten times the annual incidence of respiratory cancer in the general population would overestimate the excess deaths from this cause in this group.

In any case, the number of excess deaths, coupled with the monetary evaluation of life that OSHA may choose for policy-making purposes, must be compared with the incremental cost of preventing these excess deaths to determine whether the proposal is inflationary or anti-inflationary. Much as it may be distasteful to assign such a dollar value to human life, the policy maker implicitly does just that when he accepts or rejects some plan that, on the one hand, uses resources and, on the other hand, could save lives. Resources are not unlimited. Therefore, the truly humane decision maker will carefully calculate the amount of additional resources necessary to save one extra life under each alternative lifesaving program and will choose the program that will save a life with the least use of resources. He will continue to invest in the program until another program provides a cheaper way to save lives and so on until all the resources that society has allocated to lifesaving programs have been expended. In such manner, the policy maker maximizes the number of lives saved from any given expenditure of resources.

The analysis of benefits must show how many lives will be saved by adopting the proposed standard of 0.004 milligrams of arsenic per cubic meter of air rather than continuing the current standard of 0.5 milligrams. If the number of lives saved annually is twelve, then the cost per life saved is $111 million divided by twelve, or about $9 million. On the other hand, if the number of lives saved is 106, then the cost per life saved is about $1 million. Whether the proposal should be viewed as anti-inflationary or inflationary depends on whether the value that society places on saving a life is in excess of $1 million to $9 million or whether it is less. It will also depend on whether other projects or standards could save lives at a lower cost per life. Unfortunately, OSHA's economic analysis does not shed much light on this issue.

Analysis of Alternatives

OSHA's analysis includes estimates of the costs of two other alternatives to the existing standard: 0.1 milligrams of arsenic per cubic meter of air and 0.05 milligrams. The costs of these alternatives, as well as the cost of the proposed 0.004 standard, are summarized in Table 3–1.

TABLE 3–1

ESTIMATED COSTS OF ALTERNATIVE ARSENIC EXPOSURE STANDARDS
(millions of dollars)

Standard	Initial Costs	Annual Operating Costs	Annualized Costs
0.1 mg As/m³	40	10.7	18.4
0.05 mg As/m³	149	26.3	55.4
0.004 mg As/m³	273	56.0	111.0

SOURCE: Arthur Young and Company, *Inflationary Impact Statement: Inorganic Arsenic*, prepared for the Occupational Safety and Health Administration (April 28, 1976).

Generally, in the case of smelters, the incremental cost of moving from the 0.05-milligram level to the 0.004-milligram level is relatively low. This is because further improvements cannot be made through engineering controls, and thus compliance with the standard would be accomplished through less costly personal protective devices and revised work practices. In the case of industries that use arsenic rather than produce it (for example, the wood-preserving industry), exposure levels are currently much lower than they are in the smelters. In those cases, exposure levels can usually be lowered from 0.05 milligrams to 0.004 milligrams by using engineering controls. Therefore, the incremental cost for such industries is much higher than it is for the smelters.[12] Although OSHA attempts to estimate the costs of adopting these alternative standards, it does not consider the incremental benefits at all.

It is important to note that OSHA's analysis does not consider relying on respirators, protective garments, and revised work practices as an alternative to engineering controls where the former would be less costly. In much of the work areas of the smelters as well as at the wood-preserving and glass plants, employees would have to wear respirators and would have to rotate work assignments and work areas within each eight-hour day in order to avoid an eight-hour average exposure level that exceeds the proposed 0.004 standard. Thus, the inconvenience and loss of productivity that might accompany the wearing of respirators or the rotation of work assignments would be borne anyway in meeting the standard. Might it not be

[12] Even here, however, respirators and revised work practices would be necessary in certain instances.

less costly to permit the employer to rely entirely on respirators and work practices where feasible?

The OSHA analysis lists the types of respirators that would be required with various concentrations of inorganic arsenic. As long as the present standard of 0.5 milligrams of arsenic per cubic meter of air is met through engineering controls, there would appear to be no problem with achieving the extra measure of worker protection by means of personal protective devices and worker rotation. Since in some areas the associated expense, training, and bother associated with respirators and revised work practices would be incurred even with the maximum possible engineering controls in place, the added cost of engineering changes to achieve the proposed standard might be avoided, while achieving essentially the same results.[13] The use of respirators and protective clothing would appear to be a particularly desirable substitute for engineering controls in those high-exposure work areas that are occupied by employees for only a few hours each day.

Still another alternative not mentioned by OSHA's analysts appears worthy of consideration. Because the cost of engineering controls on *new* plant and equipment (for the purpose of meeting a prescribed level of exposure reductions) tends to be lower than retrofitting old plant and equipment, OSHA should consider tailoring the requirements accordingly. Perhaps old plants should be allowed to meet the standard through personal protection programs, and engineering controls should be required only on new plants.

Summary and Conclusion

The economic analysis submitted by OSHA appears to have adequately addressed the cost issue but has fallen short of quantifying the incremental benefits of a more stringent arsenic standard. Moreover, although the costs of meeting two alternative exposure levels have been studied, the benefits of these alternatives have been ignored so that the decision-making process could not reasonably compare the relative costs and benefits of alternative arsenic exposure standards. These inadequacies should be rectified. Specifically, OSHA should try to develop more extensive data on the relationship between exposure to arsenic and respiratory cancer. Of particular importance is detailed evidence of the effects of mild to moderate increases in exposure to arsenic over a long period of time.

---

[13] To the extent that engineering controls enabled the proposed standard to be met with less costly respirators, the net savings would be less than the cost of the engineering controls.

In the meantime, while new benefit data were being developed, OSHA would be confronted with a double-edged dilemma. It can only be surmised whether the relationship between respiratory cancer and mild overexposure to arsenic (say, concentrations of 0.004 milligrams to 0.5 milligrams) is the same as that between respiratory cancer and rather heavy overexposure to arsenic (1 milligram to 5 milligrams and above). If OSHA does not alter the present arsenic standard because of a lack of definite evidence on the danger of lower-level arsenic exposure in the workplace, lives may be lost because of additional costs of respiratory cancer each year. On the other hand, if OSHA promulgates the 0.004-milligrams standard when in fact mild overexposure to arsenic has no adverse effect on human health, then a one-time cost of $273 million will have been incurred for nought in addition to $56 million in additional annual operating expense over the time period the standard is in place.

Fortunately, there appears to be an interim option available to OSHA that minimizes the loss whether or not low-level arsenic exposure is found to be injurious to health. The relatively inexpensive use of personal protective clothing and equipment and revised work practices can be permitted as an interim measure to achieve compliance with whatever arsenic standard OSHA chooses until more definitive information about the carcinogenicity of low-level exposure to arsenic becomes available.[14] Under this option no extra lives would be placed at risk while the problem continues to be studied. At the same time, no large expenditures for engineering controls would be mandated in ignorance and fear of the unknown risks that may exist. In short, this approach minimizes the cost to society (and the inflationary effects) of addressing the problem of arsenic in the workplace.

On May 5, 1978, OSHA published the final arsenic standard, to take effect August 1, 1978.[15] The standard has been modified since the initial proposal. Instead of a permissible exposure level of 0.004 milligrams of arsenic per cubic meter of air averaged over an eight-hour period, the final regulation allows up to 0.01 milligrams. The final standard is expected to affect zinc, lead, and copper smelters only and is estimated to result in additional annual costs of $32 million.

---

[14] Of course, in some cases engineering controls would be less costly, once loss of productivity and employee morale are counted. Thus, the idea is to permit the employer to choose the less costly of the two approaches.

[15] 43 Fed. Reg. 19584 (May 5, 1978).

Industry sources, however, claim that the cost will be $94.7 million annually. The vulnerable wood-preserving industry is not covered by the standard because jurisdiction over this industry was shifted to the Department of Agriculture. The final standard, just as the proposal, requires firms to reduce arsenic exposure to the maximum degree feasible by the use of engineering controls and then to reduce exposure levels further to the prescribed levels through the use of respirators and work practice controls.

4

Exposure to Occupational Noise

John F. Morrall III

The problem with noise in the workplace is one of the most important health hazards that industry faces in terms of both costs and benefits. Unlike most other occupational health hazards, noise cuts across almost all segments of U.S. industry. This chapter attempts to assess several approaches to the solution of the occupational noise problem using the techniques of cost-effectiveness analysis.

The Occupational Safety and Health Administration (OSHA) was created as a Department of Labor agency to administer the Occupational Safety and Health Act of 1970, which was intended "to assure safe and healthful working conditions for working men and women." Under the act, the secretary of labor has the responsibility to establish and enforce safety and health standards for all enterprises engaged in interstate commerce. Included in these standards are rules related to occupational noise.

OSHA's original standard regarding occupational noise was an interim rule that limited the noise to which workers could be exposed in an eight-hour day to 90 decibels (dBA). On October 24, 1974, OSHA proposed that the 90-decibel standard be continued "until further empirical data and information on the health risk, feasibility, and economic impact indicate the practicality of an 85 dBA requirement."[1]

In its notice, OSHA also proposed specific procedures that in-

This chapter is edited from "Occupational Noise Exposure," Statement on Behalf of the Council on Wage and Price Stability before the Occupational Safety and Health Administration, Docket No. OSH-11A, September 1976.
[1] 39 Fed. Reg. 37773 (October 24, 1974).

dustry should follow in meeting the 90-decibel standard.[2] First, engineering and administrative controls should be installed to reduce workers' exposure to noise wherever feasible. Personal protective devices, such as earplugs or earmuffs, should be used only as a last resort. Second, programs are to be established for: (a) continuous monitoring of noise exposure in areas where noise levels exceed 85 decibels; (b) audiometric testing of workers exposed to noise levels in excess of 85 decibels; and (c) record keeping with respect to levels of noise exposure and worker health.

The purpose of the proposed standard is to reduce the risk of hearing loss for employees exposed to noise in the workplace for protracted periods.[3] The issue of noise is certainly a matter of concern, and improving worker health in the most efficient and effective ways is a most worthy goal. But the standard that is set should protect the maximum number of workers from hearing risk at costs that are commensurate with the full social value of that reduction in hearing risk. The standard that is adopted should be the least costly acceptable method of attaining that goal. Only then will the standard be anti-inflationary, or at least noninflationary.

OSHA had an economic analysis of the proposed regulation prepared by Bolt, Beranek and Newman, Inc., a leading consulting firm with respect to noise.[4] This economic analysis is adequate in presenting data on the costs and benefits of the proposed regulation and in discussing alternative standards, but the report is weak in analyzing the implications of the data. The present study attempts to improve on the Bolt, Beranek and Newman report by systematically comparing the benefits and costs of various portions of the proposed standard. Only through such analysis can policy makers have at hand the requisite information for making rational decisions.

After analyzing the current, proposed, and alternative standards, this study concludes that enforcing compliance with the current 90-decibel standard through engineering controls appears to be extremely costly (relative to benefits) in comparison with an enforcement program that would allow firms to employ personal protective devices

---

[2] Ibid., p. 37774.

[3] The Occupational Safety and Health Act requires the secretary of labor to "set the standard which most adequately ensures to the extent feasible, on the basis of the best available evidence, that no employee will suffer material impairment of health or functional capacity even if such employee has regular exposure . . . for the period of his working life." 29 U.S.C., section 655.

[4] Bolt, Beranek and Newman, Inc., *Economic Impact Analysis of Proposed Noise Control Regulation*, prepared for the Occupational Safety and Health Administration, April 21, 1976.

where it would be economical to do so. This study also concludes that varying the standard among industries (depending on costs and benefits) would greatly enhance the net benefits of the proposal. It suggests that OSHA consider a system of fines based on the risks of hearing impairment per plant. Such an approach might be more cost-effective than the mandated standards that are proposed.

OSHA's Analysis of Benefits

OSHA's economic analysis states that the principal benefit of the proposed standard is a reduction in hearing impairment in the work force.[5] The analysis also mentions several other possible benefits and attempts to quantify one of them—namely, reductions in workmen's compensation premiums. Two other analyses of the proposed standard have been completed—one by Nicholas A. Ashford and others,[6] and the other by Robert S. Smith.[7] These analyses attempt to measure several additional benefits of the standard, such as improvements in the work environment and the impact on worker productivity. All of these studies have shortcomings.

The present study is not the work of a hygienist or an otologist, and thus it does not address the accuracy of OSHA's estimates of the reduction in the risk of hearing impairment that would flow from promulgating the proposed standard. It does, however, address the economic implications of the proposal, based on OSHA's analysis.

Overall, the benefit section of OSHA's analysis is of high quality and of sufficient detail to allow careful, systematic analysis of various alternatives to the proposed standard. Thus, cost-effectiveness calculations can be performed in some detail.

OSHA's estimate of hearing impairment is developed over several steps. First, an estimate is made of the number of workers in the manufacturing and utilities industries who are subject to different levels of noise measured in eight-hour weighted, continuous sound levels (decibels) under alternative noise control standards. Second, the number of workers in each noise-level class is multiplied by the probability of workers' having a 25-decibel hearing threshold loss (averaged over the frequencies of 500, 1,000, and 2,000 hertz) after having worked in the presence of various levels of workplace

---

[5] Ibid.

[6] Nicholas A. Ashford and others, *Some Considerations in Choosing an Occupational Noise Exposure Regulation* (Environmental Protection Agency, 1976).

[7] Robert S. Smith, *The Occupational Safety and Health Act* (Washington, D.C.: American Enterprise Institute, 1976), chapter 3.

TABLE 4–1

SUMMARY OF INFORMATION REQUIRED FOR ESTIMATES OF BENEFITS

Sound Level Range (decibels)	Median Sound Level (decibels) (1)	Probability of Hearing Impairment: Screened Sample (percent) (2)	Percent of Workforce Exposed to Given Levels under Various Standards		
			Current (3)	90 decibels (4)	85 decibels (5)
Less than 70	60.0	0	14.5	14.5	14.5
70–75	72.5	0	15.0	14.0	14.0
75–80	77.5	0	18.5	18.5	18.5
80–85	82.5	0.5	18.5	18.5	49.4
85–90	87.5	1.5	15.1	33.9	3.0
90–95	92.5	4.8	10.8	0.2	0.2
95–100	97.5	11.0	5.8	0.2	0.2
100–105	102.5	22.0	2.2	0.2	0.2
105–110	107.5	41.0	0.6	0	0
110–115	112.5	62.0	0.04	0	0
More than 115	—	—	0	0	0
Average exposure	—	—	80.2	78.7	77.1

Dash (—): Not applicable.

NOTE: Total production workers = 12,939,300; average probability for hearing impairment = 2.21 percent; number of workers expected to suffer hearing impairment = 285,965.

SOURCE: The data are from Bolt, Beranek and Newman, Inc., *Economic Impact Analysis of Proposed Noise Control Regulation*, prepared for the Occupational Safety and Health Administration (April 21, 1976), as follows: column (2), Table 2.4; column (3), Table 2.1; columns (4) and (5), Table 2.3; and the total production worker number, Table 2.2. The rest of the information was calculated from the information in the table.

noise for twenty years. Third, the number of workers in each class under the alternative noise standards is compared to determine the number of additional workers protected from hearing impairment under alternative standards. These estimates appear in Table 4–1. Finally, the numbers are corrected for the effects of mobility, which produces a small downward adjustment in hearing impairment.[8]

OSHA provides two estimates of the risk of hearing impairment

[8] The effects of mobility are largely self-canceling because, although about 8 million more workers are exposed to noise over twenty years, the average exposure declines to about ten years.

because of noise. One study, conducted by D. W. Robinson, attempts to measure only the permanent impairment caused by noise in the workplace.[9] The other study, by W. L. Baughn, includes the impairment of hearing by all possible causes.[10] The principle of *ceteris paribus* (that is, in analyzing cause and effect, one should attempt to hold all other factors constant and isolate the effect of the variable that is relevant with respect to the particular policy) provides strong support for using the Robinson data for public policy analysis. Accordingly, this analysis relies primarily on the results of Robinson's study.[11]

A wide assortment of benefit estimates are reported by OSHA. These vary with assumptions of mobility, differences in time of exposure, differences in definition of hearing impairment, and alternative noise control standards. One weakness of the presentation is that, although there are many assessments of the benefits of *alternative* standards, no estimate of the benefits of attaining the current standard is provided. Instead, the assessments of the benefits are all in terms of *differentials* relative to Bolt, Beranek and Newman's estimate of what is feasible to achieve—not to what is being achieved relative to what ideally could be achieved.[12] This approach to estimating benefits appears to be in direct conflict with OSHA's estimate of costs, which states: "Noise control techniques and materials for quieting industrial plants are, with few exceptions, technically feasible and

---

[9] D.W. Robinson, "The Relationship between Hearing Loss and Noise Exposure," National Physical Laboratory Aero Report AC32, Teddington, England (1968).

[10] W.L. Baughn, "Relationship between Daily Noise Exposure and Hearing Loss Based on the Evaluation of 6,835 Individual Noise Exposure Cases," joint study by Environmental Protection Agency and U.S. Air Force (1973). Among the causes considered by Baughn are: workplace noise, disease, abnormalities, and intense noise and explosive sounds experienced outside the workplace. According to OSHA's economic analysis, the Baughn data also include the effects of some temporary impairment, such as the amount of impairment still present in a worker for a half hour or so after he leaves the workplace at the end of the day. See Bolt, Beranek and Newman, *Economic Impact Analysis*, p. 2-15.

[11] OSHA expressed its preference for the Robinson study as follows: "Based on these generally accepted definitions of impairment we can make an estimate of the consequences of lifelong habitual exposure at the levels which have been proposed. We have chosen for this estimate to use Robinson's data since it appears that his audiometric work is the most careful which has been done in any large study. Robinson's study has also taken some pains to eliminate such variables as temporary threshold shifts, conductive losses, and other otologic abnormalities from the data." (See 40 Fed. Reg. 12337.) Although OSHA's analysis includes the Baughn data along with the Robinson data in some tables, only the Robinson data are used in the majority of tables assessing benefits, including the workmen's compensation "benefit" estimates.

[12] See Bolt, Beranek and Newman, *Economic Impact Analysis*.

presently available."[13] It would appear, however, that enough data and explanation are present in OSHA's analysis to allow a calculation of the benefits of enforcing the present standard. These calculations are shown later in this study.

Besides calculating the additional number of workers protected from hearing impairment by an 85-decibel standard over a 90-decibel level, the OSHA analysis calculated the potential additional benefits of reduced workmen's compensation payments.[14] Although this is an interesting exercise, it needlessly complicates the analysis because it is irrelevant to a cost-benefit calculation. A reduction in workmen's compensation payments is a benefit to employers who no longer have to pay workmen's compensation premiums, but this represents an almost equal and offsetting cost to workers who no longer receive such payments.[15] The net benefits workers receive are the reduction in the risk of hearing impairment minus the workmen's compensation payments they would have received.[16]

Other benefits mentioned in OSHA's study include reductions in occupational injuries and workplace absenteeism, and improvements in work productivity. Because of the lack of data and demonstrable relationships, however, the OSHA analysis mentions these factors only as unconfirmed hypotheses requiring additional work. The one scientific study that the OSHA report mentions in support of these hypotheses uses hearing protectors to reduce the level of noise exposure.[17] Probably the best way to approach the issue of additional, unquantified benefits is to consider them separately. This procedure, which was followed in both the Smith and the Ashford studies, will be attempted later in this study.

It should be emphasized that, with the few exceptions mentioned above, the OSHA's analysis of benefits appears to be excellent. It certainly provides, to the extent practical, quantitative estimates of benefits. Where it falls short is in relating those benefits to costs and in using as the basis for comparison a hypothetical, partial compliance with the present standard.

---

[13] Ibid., p. 3-11. This section on benefits estimates that, if all feasible engineering and administrative controls were installed, 77,636 (that is, 0.6 percent) workers would still not be protected from a 90-decibel noise level; see ibid., p. 2-11.

[14] Ibid., p. 2-30.

[15] To the extent that administrative costs are saved or that premiums do not match payments, these benefits should be included; the relative magnitudes, however, are small enough to ignore.

[16] Of course, there are redistributional aspects of workmen's compensation.

[17] Bolt, Beranek and Newman, *Economic Impact Analysis*, p. 2-41.

TABLE 4–2

ESTIMATED NUMBER OF WORKERS HAVING A HEARING THRESHOLD LOSS
OF 25 DECIBELS OR MORE AFTER TWENTY YEARS OF EXPOSURE TO
WORKPLACE NOISE ALONE, UNDER SEVERAL POSSIBLE REGULATIONS

Regulation[a]	Percent of Workers	Number of Workers
90/—	0.67	86,400
90/90	0.61	74,300
85/—	0.34	44,400
85/85	0.26	33,800
90/85	0.23	30,000
90/80	0.17	21,900
85/80	0.09	11,400

NOTE: The hearing threshold loss of 25 decibels or more is averaged over 500, 1,000, and 2,000 hertz.

[a] In each regulation category, the first number indicates the noise level for the initiation of engineering and administrative controls. The second number indicates the noise level for the use of hearing protectors with the assumption that 75 percent of the workers required to wear protectors would do so and would wear them correctly.

SOURCE: Bolt, Beranek and Newman, Inc., *Economic Impact Analysis*, Table 2.14.

Table 4–2 presents the report's best estimate of the benefits obtainable under several possible regulations. The best definitions, data, and estimates are used to show the range of benefits. They range from protecting all but 86,400 workers from a 25-decibel hearing loss after twenty years of exposure to workplace noise under the current standard (assuming full compliance) to protecting all but 11,400 workers under a combined standard whereby engineering and administrative controls are required at 85 decibels and hearing protectors and audiometric testing are required at 80 decibels.

In calculating this range, it is assumed that hearing protectors are 75 percent effective. The estimate of 75 percent effectiveness is the low estimate reported by OSHA. The report states: "A promulgated regulation including credible evidence of strong enforcement, with significant penalties, would result in a condition that lies between the 'first' (100 percent effectiveness) and the 'second' condition (75 percent effectiveness)."[18] These data will be used later as part of the benefit-cost estimates.

---

[18] Ibid., p. 2-35.

OSHA's Analysis of Costs

OSHA's economic analysis provides detailed estimates of the one-time capital costs of the noise-abatement and administrative procedures that likely would be utilized if the proposal were promulgated in its present form. The accuracy of these industry-by-industry estimates is not addressed here; that is a matter for acoustical engineers to determine. Certain economic ramifications of these estimates are, however, treated.

OSHA's estimate is that full compliance with the current 90-decibel standard would produce capital costs of $10.5 billion for equipment with an average life of twenty years, the same period over which the benefits were calculated. Full compliance with the 85-decibel standard would generate an additional $8 billion in capital costs.[19] The study also estimates that the annual cost of maintaining noise control equipment would be approximately 5 percent of the capital costs.[20] In addition, OSHA estimates that about $155 million a year would be required for monitoring, record keeping, and associated tasks for the estimated 12,939,300 production workers in manufacturing and public utilities.[21] Audiometric testing—including depreciation, costs of equipment, personnel, and lost production time—is estimated at $20 per production worker, while use of hearing protectors would add another $10 per production worker.[22]

Besides these estimates, which are based on full compliance within five years, OSHA also presents ten-year and fifteen-year compliance scenarios. The five-year compliance period estimates are based on the assumption that retrofit of existing plants would be required, whereas the ten-year and fifteen-year periods assume that the phasing in of new, quieter equipment would occur through normal capital replacement at a cost-reduction rate of 3 percent a year. This latter assumption produces a cost figure for the ten-year period of 82 percent of that for the five-year period. For the fifteen-year period, the cost figure is 75 percent of that for the five-year period.

One weakness of OSHA's cost analysis is that their analysis does not group these costs for purposes of comparison with the options discussed in the section on benefits. This study attempts to

---

[19] Ibid., p. 3-1. "Full" compliance does not mean perfect compliance inasmuch as the benefit section of the OSHA analysis estimates that from 0.6 to 3.6 percent of workers would not be adequately protected by the 90-decibel and the 85-decibel engineering standards.

[20] Ibid., p. 3-34.

[21] Ibid., p. 3-8.

[22] Ibid., pp. 3-9 and 3-33.

make such a grouping and explicitly to compare the total cost estimates with the total benefit estimates for the various proposed standards.

OSHA's Cost-Benefit Analysis

In this section, OSHA's best-data estimates of costs and benefits are used to compare the benefits and the costs of OSHA's proposed standard. Both the study by Ashford and others and the study by Smith attempt formal cost-benefit analysis of the proposed 90-decibel and 85-decibel standards. The Ashford study concludes:

> The accounting suggested indicates that compliance with a 90 dBA standard is likely to yield a net benefit to society even after ten years. Compliance with 85 dBA appears to be achievable at a net cost after ten years, but at a figure very much smaller than the compliance cost estimates. Ultimately, compliance with the 85 dBA standard is a net benefit to society.[23]

On the other hand, the Smith study concludes:

> Based on this analysis, I conjecture that workers would not be willing to pay the costs of either the 90- or 85-decibel noise abatement programs. Because the beneficiaries would probably rather spend the $13.5 or $31.6 on other goods or services, OSHA should not enforce either standard.[24]

Both studies are based on Bolt, Beranek and Newman's earlier estimates,[25] which have been superseded by the new estimates provided by the firm in doing OSHA's analysis. The present analysis uses Bolt, Beranek and Newman's latest data.

Table 4–2 portrays the major alternative standards considered in the benefits section of OSHA's study. So that benefits and costs can be compared, the costs associated with the alternative standards must be determined. This exercise is straightforward, and the results are shown in Table 4–3. The gross (total) cost estimates are based on the addition of the capital cost estimate of $10.5 billion for the 90-decibel standard and $18.5 billion for the 85-decibel standard plus the present value of 5 percent of the capital costs per year for twenty

[23] Ashford and others, *Some Considerations in Choosing an Occupational Noise Exposure Regulation,* p. 2-60.

[24] Smith, *The Occupational Safety and Health Act,* p. 56.

[25] R.D. Bruce and others, *Impact of Noise Control at the Workplace,* Bolt, Beranek and Newman, Inc., Report No. 2671, submitted to the Occupational Safety and Health Administration, January 1974.

TABLE 4-3

Gross Total, Average, and Marginal Costs per Worker Protected from a 25-Decibel Hearing Impairment for Various Regulations

Regulation[a]	Number of Workers Protected (thousands) (1)	Total Gross Costs (billions of dollars) (2)	Additional Workers Protected (thousands) (3)	Additional Gross Costs (billions of dollars) (4)	Average Gross Costs (dollars) (5)	Marginal Gross Costs (dollars) (6)
Current conditions	0	0	0	...	...	...
—/90	184.4	1.9	184.4	1.9	10,304	10,304
90/—	199.6	16.2	15.2	14.3	81,656	940,789
—/85	205.9	2.4	21.5[b]	0.5[b]	11,656	23,256[b]
90/90	206.7	16.8	0.8	14.4	81,277	18,000,000
—/80	214.5	3.1	8.6[c]	0.7[c]	14,452	81,395[c]
85/—	241.5	27.7	27.0	24.6	114,700	911,111
85/85	253.0	28.8	11.5	1.1	113,833	95,652
90/85	256.0	17.3	41.5[d]	14.2[d]	67,573	342,169[d]
90/80	264.1	18.0	8.1	0.7	68,156	86,420
90/80	264.1	18.0	49.6[d]	14.9[d]	68,156	300,403[d]
85/80	274.6	29.5	10.5	11.8	107,429	1,095,238

[a] In each regulation category, the first number indicates the noise level for the initiation of engineering and administrative controls. The second number indicates the noise level for the use of hearing protector with the assumption that 75 percent of the workers required to wear protectors would do so and would wear them correctly.

[b] Calculated relative to regulation —/90.

[c] Calculated relative to regulation —/85.

[d] Calculated relative to regulation —/80.

SOURCE: Column (1) was calculated by subtracting the estimated number of workers impaired under the various regulations found in Table 4-2 from the estimated number impaired under present conditions, 286,000; column (2) was calculated from data supplied in OSHA's economic analysis as explained in the text; column (3) was calculated by subtracting from the number in column (1) the number from the previous regulation in column (1), unless otherwise noted; column (4) was calculated from column (2) in the same manner as column (3); column (5) equals column (2) divided by column (1); and column (6) equals column (4) divided by column (3).

years using a 10 percent discount rate, which represents OSHA's estimate of maintenance costs. To this sum, $1.3 billion is added, which represents the present value of the estimated $155 million annual cost for noise monitoring for 13 million workers. Added in next is the present value of twenty years of annual costs for the noise-monitoring and hearing-protector program. This estimate varies with the action level and the number of workers in the program, and it is calculated from the data in Table 4–1. Those data are used to estimate the number of workers exposed to the various decibel levels under the alternative standards that would require audiometric testing and hearing protectors. As stated above, OSHA's estimates are $20 a year per person for the audiometric-testing program and $10 a year per person for hearing protectors. The present values were in all cases discounted at 10 percent a year.

Besides the options listed in Table 4–2, Table 4–3 lists three additional options: hearing protectors, audiometric testing, and noise monitoring at 80 decibels, at 85 decibels, and at 90 decibels. As with the options originally listed in Table 4–2, the three additional options are based on the conservative assumption that the hearing-protector and audiometric-testing programs would be 75 percent effective.

The options are listed in Table 4–3 in increasing order of the number of workers protected from hearing impairment. In order to make these rankings, it was necessary first to calculate the estimated number of workers impaired after twenty years of exposure to current workplace noise levels. This estimate, although not in OSHA's analysis, can be calculated from the data in Table 4–1. This calculation produces an estimate of 286,000 workers who would be impaired after twenty years under the present, imperfectly enforced standard. The number of workers protected by each standard is reported in column 2; it was calculated by subtracting the number of workers with hearing losses reported in Table 4–2 for each standard from the 286,000 impaired under present enforcement levels. The benefit estimates for the three hearing-protector standards were calculated from data in Table 4–1.

In determining the socially optimum standard in cost-benefit analysis, the rule is to choose the standard that maximizes net benefits (that is, benefits minus costs). In this instance, however, a good estimate of the dollar benefits of not having a hearing impairment after twenty years of exposure is not available. The best that can be done is to present the values implied by the various policy options and let the policy maker (in this case, the secretary of labor) choose the option. This is thus a case of using cost-effectiveness analysis as opposed to cost-benefit analysis.

The first step in the analysis is to eliminate the options that are not cost-effective relative to some other option. To determine which are not cost-effective, the marginal (additional) cost per additional worker protected with each increasingly stringent standard must be calculated. Whenever marginal costs decline (that is, it costs less to protect one more worker than to protect the previous worker), one should reject the weaker standard in favor of the standard offering more protection. A quick glance at columns 2 and 3 in Table 4–3 reveals several standards that fail this test because the next more stringent standard can be achieved at negative marginal costs (that is, more total protection is offered at less total cost). By this criterion, the 90-decibel engineering option, the 90-decibel engineering and hearing-protector option, the 85-decibel engineering option, and the 85-decibel engineering and hearing-protector option should be eliminated from further consideration because in each case there exists a standard that is both more cost-effective and more stringent.

There is one other standard listed in Table 4–3 that should be eliminated by similar reasoning, but this is more difficult to see until the actual ratios of marginal costs to workers protected are calculated. Columns 4 and 5 show the additional workers protected and the additional costs relative to the previous, less stringent standard that was not eliminated above. Column 7 shows the marginal costs per additional worker protected. Ignoring the standards that have been eliminated, marginal cost rises steadily as more and more workers are protected until, at 90/80 relative to 90/85 (that is, the 90-decibel engineering plus the 80-decibel hearing-protector option relative to the 90-decibel engineering plus the 85-decibel hearing-protector option), marginal cost declines from $342,169 per worker to $86,420. Thus, the 90/85 standard also should be eliminated because there is a more stringent standard that can be obtained at lower marginal cost. Eliminating this option requires a recalculation of the marginal cost of the 90/80 standard, this time relative to the —/80 standard (that is, the standard requiring hearing protectors at 80 decibels). The new marginal cost figure shown in Table 4–3 is $300,403.

The elimination of the standards that are not cost-effective leaves six cost-effective standards—namely, the current standard; the 90-decibel, 85-decibel, and 80-decibel hearing-protector options; and the 90/80 and 85/80 combination options. These standards and their marginal and average costs are illustrated in Figure 4–1. Only one of these six cost-effective standards will be the most cost-beneficial, but determining which one that is requires knowledge of the value today of protecting a person from hearing impairment twenty years from now.

If policy makers have an idea of the value of avoiding hearing impairment, they may select the most cost-beneficial (that is, the least inflationary) approach by selecting the option in which marginal costs equal that value.[26] In terms of Figure 4–1, the policy maker must draw a horizontal line that corresponds to this dollar evaluation. The intersection point determines the cost-beneficial standard.

Even if policy makers have no idea what the value of hearing impairment is, the very act of choosing among these policy options places an implicit value on hearing loss. For example, choosing the 90/80 option means that OSHA implicitly believes that preventing hearing loss is equal to $300,403, but not $300,404.

Although data have been presented on only six options (including the option of doing nothing), it is clear from the nature of the standards that options in between these six could be promulgated. For example, hearing protectors could be required at 89 decibels, or engineering controls, in conjunction with hearing protectors at 80 decibels, could be required at 89 decibels, and so forth. Since everyone who properly wears hearing protectors at 80 decibels is protected from hearing loss, lowering the hearing-protector level further is obviously not cost-effective (although more stringent enforcement and educational programs might be). Because marginal costs appear to increase rapidly with the use of engineering controls, if it is decided that hearing loss is worth more than $89,395 per person protected, then simply extrapolating between the options in Figure 4–1 is probably not prudent. Empirical evidence on additional options such as 93 and 87 decibels might be desirable.

The above estimates represent the proper way to view the problem of determining the workplace noise standard that is most cost-beneficial, given the data presented in OSHA's analysis and incorporating OSHA's preferred estimates of benefits and definitions. These cost-benefit estimates, however, seem to be biased upward because OSHA was not able to quantify all of the potential benefits of the standard. Part of the reason, apparently, is that in some cases the benefits are so small that it is hard to verify their existence empirically. The way to proceed in such situations is to determine whether making assumptions about these intangible benefits makes much difference in the results of the analysis based on the hard data.

---

[26] Assuming that the value of everyone's hearing is equal.

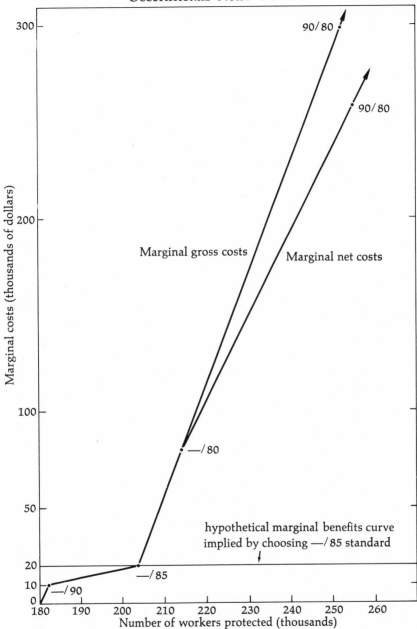

FIGURE 4–1
COMPARISON OF COST-EFFECTIVE STANDARDS FOR
OCCUPATIONAL NOISE EXPOSURE

NOTE: The coordinates for marginal gross costs at 85/80 are $1.1 million and 275,000 workers; for marginal net costs at 85/80, $0.7 million and 275,000 workers.
SOURCE: Column (6) from Tables 4–3 and 4–4; only "cost-effective" options considered.

An attempt will be made to bias the results in favor of engineering controls since Table 4–3 and Figure 4–1 appear to support the use of hearing protectors. It will be assumed that the additional benefits all accrue to the approach by way of engineering and administrative controls as opposed to the approach by way of personal protection. Some increase in costs, however, should be attributed to the fact that hearing protectors are uncomfortable. The assumption that all the intangible benefits accrue to the engineering-only standards implies that the intangible benefits of wearing hearing protectors are equal to, if not greater than, their discomfort costs.

First, it is clear that some workers would be willing to accept lower wages if they could work in more pleasant surroundings. Certainly, excessive noise is one of the conditions that cause annoyance, and workers would be willing to pay some amount to eliminate it. Theoretically, one should be able to infer what that amount might be from differences in wage rates among jobs identical except for the noise factor. Good data on this issue are not available, however.[27]

Robert S. Smith has attempted to estimate the value of the reduction of workplace noise by examining the evidence on what property owners are willing to pay for similar reductions in noise levels caused by airplanes and traffic.[28] Two of the best and most recent studies utilizing this approach summarize the results of previous work and present original work of their own.[29] The consensus estimate of the effect on property value is that a 1-decibel reduction produces a 0.5 percent increase in property values. Assuming a medium residential property value of $30,000 (this includes apartments), a 1-decibel reduction would be worth $150 per household. Using this estimate per worker should produce an estimate that is biased upward because the average household contains about three members and, it is presumed, benefits to all are reflected in property values.[30]

The next step is to calculate the average reduction in noise levels using the data in Table 4–1. Separate calculations show that enforce-

---

[27] The existence of these differences in wage rates does not mean that the benefits of the reduction in noise should be discounted because, if such differences do exist, a reduction in noise would likely lead to a reduction in money wages and an offset to the cost of reducing the noise. If they do exist, however, and fully compensate for the annoyance factor, then the rationale for the standard must rest on workers' ignorance of the health effects.

[28] See Smith, *The Occupational Safety and Health Act*, pp. 46–52.

[29] See A.A. Walters, *Noise and Prices* (London: Oxford University Press, 1975); and J.P. Nelson, *Effects of Mobile Source Air and Noise Pollution on Residential Property Values* (University Park: Pennsylvania State University, Institute for Research on Human Resources, 1975).

[30] There are other reasons this estimate overstates a worker's willingness to pay for noise reductions in the workplace. For example, Smith cites a study that

ment of the present 90-decibel engineering standard would lead to a 1.5-decibel reduction, whereas the proposed 85-decibel engineering standard would produce an additional 1.6-decibel reduction. Multiplying the decibel reductions times the 12,939,300 workers in manufacturing times the $150 per decibel estimate produces a gain of $2.9 billion for the 90-decibel standard and $6.0 billion for the 85-decibel standard. It should be noted, however, that these are capital costs and therefore again overstate true benefits because the time period (for both costs and benefits) is only twenty years.

The second type of benefits that might be measured are the benefits from reduced absenteeism.[31] This estimate will be biased upward. First, the estimate may involve a bit of double counting because one possible reason that workers stay home is that they do not like the noisy working conditions, and a value has already been computed for that factor. Second, if quieter working conditions reduce absenteeism, workers must give up leisure, which presumably has some value to them. Third, as OSHA's report points out, there is no conclusive evidence that absenteeism is caused by excessive noise.

Nevertheless, an attempt has been made to include this possible benefit by calculating the average wage paid per eight-hour day in manufacturing in 1975 and adding to this figure an estimate of the training and turnover costs specific to the worker. This produces an estimate that an extra one day's absence by a worker costs the firm $42.32.[32] Next, it is assumed that, for the workers in the interval of 85 decibels to 90 decibels, a reduction in noise to 85 decibels would reduce working absenteeism by one day a year; for workers in the group over 90 decibels, it is assumed that absenteeism would decline by two days a year.[33] The $42.32 a day is then multiplied by the 2.43

---

shows people are more annoyed by neighborhood noise than workplace noise and that around airports they are more bothered by television interference and the possibility of airplane crashes than by aircraft noise. Also, noted authority E.J. Mishan argues that these studies overestimate the social cost of noise. See E.J. Mishan, *Cost-Benefit Analysis*, 2nd ed. (London: Allen University, 1975).

[31] Ashford and others have previously attempted to quantify this effect using the first results of Bolt, Beranek and Newman. Unfortunately, their attempt is marred by methodological problems such as the use of a $10 billion gross national product (GNP) figure for reducing one day's absenteeism, which implies a total GNP for 1965 of more than $2.5 trillion. See Ashford and others, *Some Considerations in Choosing an Occupational Noise Exposure Regulation*, p. 2-55.

[32] This figure is calculated by multiplying the average hourly earnings in manufacturing in 1975 ($4.81) by eight hours a day and by 1.10 to take account of training and turnover costs associated with replacing workers.

[33] Current absenteeism is about six days a year. The absenteeism assumptions in this paper imply that every 5-decibel reduction reduces absenteeism by about 17 percent. This is probably an overestimate because it is likely that a relationship of this magnitude would have been firmly established by previous research.

million man-days that would be saved by a 90-decibel standard and the 6.42 million man-days saved by an 85-decibel standard to produce benefit estimates of $102.8 million and $271.7 million a year, respectively. The number of workers removed from the relevant intervals by each standard was calculated from the data in Table 4–1.

The present value of the twenty-year flow of benefits was calculated using a 10 percent discount rate, as before, to produce capitalized estimates of $875 million and $2,313 million, respectively. These estimates, along with the estimates of $2.9 billion and $6.0 billion for the benefits from reduction in annoyance, were then subtracted from the relevant numbers in column 3 of Table 4–3 to produce a new total net cost column in Table 4–4, which is otherwise calculated the same way as Table 4–3.

Using the same logic as before, we can again examine the various options for cost-effectiveness and then policy makers can determine the standard that is most cost-beneficial. The results of Table 4–4 do not differ much from the results of Table 4–3, except that the marginal cost estimate for the 90/80 standard is reduced from $300,403 to $223,790 and the estimate for the 85/90 standard is reduced from more than $1 million to $666,667. The same standards that were dropped before have to be eliminated this time, because other standards protect more workers at less additional costs per worker, and, since no additional benefits are attributed to the hearing-protector standards, no changes are made in the estimates of marginal costs.

Because the estimates of benefits are biased upward, and the results are biased in favor of engineering and administrative controls (as opposed to hearing-protector standards),[34] the lack of any significant effect of this exercise seems to lend support to the option of hearing-protector standards, unless the value of protecting an individual from hearing impairment twenty years from now is placed near $223,000. The effect of compounding over twenty years should also be noted. One relevant question is whether a worker today would be willing to put up with a 25-decibel hearing loss twenty years from now in exchange for a cash payment of more than $1.5 million.[35] This is a relevant question because, if a worker would accept anything less, employers (and, ultimately, consumers) could reduce total costs while making employees better off than with the 90/80 option.

---

[34] In addition to not counting any of the potential benefits of the hearing-protector standards, despite findings that such a program does lead to benefits, this study has also chosen OSHA's lower-bound estimate of the effectiveness of hearing protectors.

[35] A discount rate of 10 percent is used, as in all previous calculations.

In summary, it appears that some variant that allows the option of compliance through use of hearing protectors and audiometric-testing programs with strong incentives for enforcement is likely to be the most cost-beneficial, and therefore the most anti-inflationary, approach to the problem. If this type of program can be made more than 75 percent effective, the advantage increases tremendously. This is true even relative to enforcing the current 90-decibel standard requiring engineering and administrative controls.

Alternatives

If OSHA rejects the hearing-protector approach to reduced hearing impairment suggested in the previous section, the high costs of engineering and administrative standards call for consideration of additional alternatives. Although OSHA's analysis does not systematically compare costs and benefits, enough information is presented so that the cost-effectiveness of several alternatives can be explored.

For example, options that the OSHA analysis did not consider include the use of hearing protectors to comply with the standard and the continuation of the status quo. Options that the OSHA analysis did review on either the cost or the benefit side (but not both) include various combinations of engineering and hearing-protector standards as listed in Table 4–3 and compliance over five, ten, or fifteen years.

In view of the findings in Tables 4–3 and 4–4, an immediate imposition of a hearing-protector and audiometric-testing program, coupled with a ten-year or fifteen-year compliance period for engineering and administrative controls would be more cost-effective than the five-year standard. This is because the hearing-protector portion of the standard provides most of the coverage immediately at reasonable costs, whereas the additional coverage provided by the engineering controls comes at extremely high marginal costs. It is also likely that technological change stimulated by the demand for noise-abatement equipment will, given enough time, cause the real cost of quiet machinery to decline at a higher rate than the 3 percent reduction rate assumed in the OSHA analysis. Conversely, OSHA should consider the possibility that over fifteen years medical technology could advance far enough either to prevent or to alleviate this type of hearing impairment. These considerations lend strong support to the options that include longer compliance periods.

Another alternative or variation not considered in the OSHA

TABLE 4-4

Net Total, Average, and Marginal Costs per Worker Protected from a 25-Decibel Hearing Impairment for Various Regulations

Regulation[a]	Number of Workers Protected (thousands) (1)	Total Net Costs (billions of dollars) (2)	Additional Workers Protected (thousands) (3)	Additional Net Costs (billions of dollars) (4)	Average Net Costs (dollars) (5)	Marginal Net Costs (dollars) (6)
Current conditions	0	0	0	0	—	—
—/90	184.4	1.9	184.9	1.9	10,304	10,304
90/—	199.6	12.4	15.2	10.5	62,124	690,789
—/85	205.9	2.4	21.5[b]	0.5[b]	11,656	23,256[b]
90/90	206.7	13.0	0.8	10.6	62,289	13,250,000
—/80	214.5	3.1	8.6[c]	0.7[c]	14,452	81,395[c]
85/—	241.5	19.4	27.0	16.3	80,033	603,704
85/85	253.0	20.5	11.5	1.1	81,103	95,652
90/85	256.0	13.5	41.5[d]	10.4[d]	52,734	250,602[d]
90/80	264.1	14.2	8.1	0.7	53,377	86,420
90/80	264.1	14.2	49.6[d]	11.1[d]	53,377	223,790[d]
85/80	274.6	21.2	10.5	7.0	77,720	666,667

Dash (—): Not applicable.

[a] In each regulation category, the first number indicates the noise level for the initiation of engineering and administrative controls. The second number indicates the noise level for the use of hearing protectors with the assumption that 75 percent of the workers required to wear protectors would do so and would wear them correctly.

[b] Calculated relative to regulation —/90.

[c] Calculated relative to regulation —/85.

[d] Calculated relative to regulation —/80.

SOURCE: Column (2) was calculated as in Table 4-3 except that the estimates for the benefits of the potential reduction in absenteeism and annoyance were subtracted from the gross cost estimates in Table 4-3, column (2). The estimates of potential benefits are described in the text. The rest of the calculations are the same as in Table 4-3.

TABLE 4–5

Gross and Net Costs of Several Regulations by Two-Digit SIC Industries
(thousands of dollars)

SIC Code	Gross Costs per Worker Protected		Net Costs per Worker Protected	
	90/—	85/—	90/—	85/—
20	49.9	119.0	39.2	83.3
21	68.9	132.5	54.1	92.7
22	150.9	262.8	118.6	184.0
24	151.5	202.0	119.0	141.4
24	99.9	100.5	78.5	70.3[a]
26	41.1	51.9	32.3	36.3
27	71.6	143.1	56.3	100.2
28	52.8	88.1	41.5	61.7
29	143.1	171.2	112.4	119.8
30	25.1	44.9	19.7	31.4
32	34.7	64.1	27.3	44.9
33	144.6	248.0	113.7	174.6
34	128.0	125.2	110.6	87.6[a]
35	154.8	163.1	121.7	114.2[a]
36	12.4	25.8	9.8	18.0
37	57.9	74.2	45.5	52.0
49	91.0	126.4	71.5	88.5
Weighted average	81.2	114.7	62.1	80.0

[a] Since in these industries the net cost of the 85/— standard is less than that of the 90/— standard, the 85/— standard is more cost-effective than the 90/— standard (that is, the marginal cost of attaining the more protective standard is negative). Therefore, the 90/— standard for those industries should automatically be rejected in favor of the stricter regulation.

Source: Calculated from data in the appendix to OSHA's economic analysis, adjusted by the cost estimates in Tables 4-3 and 4-4, and assuming that hearing risk for each industry equals the national average.

analysis is that of industry-by-industry standards. Table 4–5 computes for several industries (identified by two-digit Standard Industrial Classifications) the gross and net costs per worker protected from a hearing loss by the 90-decibel and 85-decibel engineering standards. The gross cost per worker protected by the 90-decibel engineering-only standard ranges from $12,446 for SIC 36 (electrical machinery) to $154,840 for SIC 35 (nonelectrical machinery), with an industrywide average of $81,162 per worker.[36] The costs for SIC 22 (textiles), 24 (lumber), 29 (petroleum refining), and 33 (primary metals) are also more than $140,000 per worker protected. For the 85-decibel engineering-only standard, similar disparities appear. The range is from $25,760 for electrical machinery to $262,800 for textiles, with an industrywide average of $114,700.

These data indicate that standards that vary by industry could protect more workers for less cost than industrywide standards. For example, for the same cost more than twelve times as many workers could be protected with a 90-decibel standard in the electrical machinery industry as could be protected in the textiles, lumber, primary metals, or nonelectrical machinery industries. Another way to view the data is that an 85-decibel standard in seven industries could protect more workers at less cost than it would take to protect workers in the textiles, lumber, or nonelectrical machinery industries with a 90-decibel standard. It is also apparent, especially using the net cost data, that the engineering-only standards would be more cost-effective for some industries than the hearing-protector standards are for others. Thus, overall cost-effectiveness could be improved by requiring (or allowing) engineering controls in some industries.[37] Obviously, there are all sorts of possible adjustments that would protect more workers at less extra costs beginning from various starting points.

As was suggested earlier, the approach that should be used to find the most cost-effective combination is for policy makers to agree upon a value for protecting hearing loss per person and to rank the standards for each industry by increasing marginal costs. The cost-effective standard for each industry is then determined by using the rule that marginal social benefits (that is, the evaluation of the worth of protecting hearing loss) equal marginal costs. Alternatively, different benefit levels could be chosen and, for each level, the optimum combination of standards for each industry could be solved and the total number of workers and costs calculated. On the basis of this information, a given cost-effective set of standards could be chosen and an implicit benefit level would result.

Such industry-by-industry calculations seem to offer opportunities for large cost savings for protecting a given number of

---

[36] These calculations are based on the assumption that workers in different industries are subject to the same probability of hearing loss. Before policy is based on these figures, calculations of risk should be made industry by industry.

[37] This result follows because the 90-decibel engineering standard for SIC 36 shows lower net costs than the industry average net cost for the 90-decibel hearing-protector standard (see Table 4-4).

workers or for being able to protect a substantially greater number of workers for the same expenditure. In making such calculations, the possible additional administrative costs should be considered. The argument that this approach is inequitable because different groups of workers would be protected from hearing loss in different degrees appears fallacious, since a worker's well-being depends upon more than just the risk of hearing loss. It also depends upon the worker's attitude toward risk-taking and upon his money wages. The approach outlined here would allow such adjustments to offset the unequal risks. In addition, there would appear to be something fundamentally inequitable about adopting a policy that would protect fewer workers for the same cost instead of one that would protect more workers at less or equal cost.

If the industry-by-industry approach would produce more cost-effective protection against hearing impairment at the two-digit SIC level, then it presumably would produce even greater cost savings at the three-digit SIC level (disregarding administrative costs for the moment). For example, at the three-digit level, the range of costs per worker protected with the 90-decibel engineering-only standard varies from $980 for several industries in the electrical machinery and transportation groups to $705,600 for metal forging and stamping. There would likely be even greater variation in costs per worker protected and therefore greater cost savings if different standards were set at the four-digit or five-digit SIC levels, or even if different standards were set at separate work areas.

Of course, at this point the administrative costs loom large. If, however, some simple system could be found to create incentives at the firm and plant levels to protect workers from hearing impairment at the level of protection determined by OSHA, the potential cost savings might be extremely high.

To some extent the existence of wage differentials, good management, and the workmen's compensation program when plants are experience-rated creates such an incentive. But probably this incentive is not strong enough. If it is not, two possible approaches are suggested for further consideration by OSHA. Both require that policy makers explicitly determine the value of protecting the average worker from hearing impairment. Since it is clear that setting a standard implicitly assigns a value to hearing loss, an explicit determination would require no more information than the implicit one.

Once the appropriate benefit level is chosen, either a self-insuring workmen's compensation system with fixed rewards could be used to compensate workers or OSHA could set a yearly fine per plant based on the number of workers in the plant, the probability that they would experience a hearing impairment after twenty years, and the twenty-year annuity rate of the chosen benefit level. For example, at present national average noise levels, a plant with 1,000 workers would have about twenty-two workers suffering hearing impairment after twenty years. If OSHA were about to decide on the 90/80 industrywide option, the implicit value placed on hearing would be $86,420 per worker. If a 10 percent discount rate is used to calculate the tax, this plant would be fined $223,396 a year until it either reduced the level of workplace noise or instigated an effective hearing-protector program. It seems clear that a fine of this size would create strong incentives for management to reduce the burden of fines by reducing workplace noise.

This system would also protect more workers at less cost than an industrywide 90/80 standard. Different plants would attempt to reduce the tax by probably as many different ways as there are plants. Each plant manager would attempt to reduce the number of workers subject to hearing loss until the cost of such reduction equaled $10,154 a year, the annuity payment for the $86,420 valuation.

This system would require that plant managers keep records of the exposure of employees to noise and of the effectiveness of the hearing-protector program. But this is something that the proposed standards would also require. Thus, the additional administrative costs of the fine approach versus the single-standard approach should not be large. Certainly, this approach to protecting workers deserves consideration by OSHA—if not now, then in the future.

Conclusion and Recommendations

OSHA's analysis of the proposed noise standard provides a wealth of information on costs, benefits, and alternatives that can be used to estimate the possible inflationary consequences of the proposal and of several alternative actions. The major criticism is that, although most of the information is there, OSHA's report contains no systematic cost-benefit analysis and very little systematic cost-effectiveness analysis. The present study has attempted to remedy this situation by choosing the assumptions and definitions that OSHA appears to prefer and using what is believed to be the correct methodology to analyze systematically the various options and to pose the policy questions in the most direct manner. The various combinations or alternatives have not been exhausted, nor have all the calculations been completed. OSHA should take these next steps before promulgating a final standard.

This study has not attempted to enter into the fields of industrial engineering and otology; it has not questioned the basic data estimates presented in OSHA's analysis. To the extent that future evidence affects the validity of the estimates, the basic findings of this study might change. Nevertheless, the methodology of cost-benefit analysis and the economics used in the calculations should stand invariant to changes in assumptions and could be used to recompute the calculations.

Based on these calculations and findings, several conclusions can reasonably be made with respect to the proposed noise standards. It appears from both Table 4–3 and Table 4–4 that an effectively administered hearing-protector program could provide most of the benefits at much lower cost in comparison with an industrywide engineering-only noise standard set at either a 90-decibel or an 85-decibel level or used in combination with the various hearing-protector standards. In fact, some may wonder why OSHA has not immediately adopted an 85-decibel hearing-protector standard, in view of the relatively reasonable marginal cost of about $23,000 per hearing impairment avoided. The question looms even larger when one considers that the present analysis was biased against the hearing-protector standard. For example, if either part of the $8.3 billion in potential benefits from the reduction in absenteeism or annoyance assigned to the 85-decibel engineering standard could be applied to the $2.4 billion estimated cost of a hearing-protector and audiometric-testing program, or if the effectiveness of such a program could be increased above 75 percent, the marginal cost of the standard would quickly fall to compellingly low levels.

OSHA should consider the option of allowing hearing protectors to be used in complying with whatever standard is finally set. If a final hearing-protector standard is unacceptable to OSHA, the hearing-protector option is particularly well suited for an interim standard that could be set while OSHA considers some of the additional alternatives proposed here. These include implementing industry-by-industry standards at the two-digit or three-digit SIC level, allowing longer compliance periods, or using fines or a workmen's compensation-type system to create incentives at a very decentralized level.

The occupational noise exposure regulation first proposed on October 24, 1974, has not yet been promulgated. OSHA continues working to develop the final standard while stepping up enforcement of the existing standard.

PART TWO

Product Safety

5

Lawn Mower Safety

Thomas M. Lenard

The Consumer Product Safety Commission (CPSC), which was created by legislation in October 1972, has primary responsibility for mandating safety standards to reduce the unreasonable risk of injury from consumer products. The commission has been subject to substantial criticism reflecting different points of view—some complain that it is not doing enough, while others complain that it is doing too much. If promulgated, the lawn mower safety standard would be the most costly standard thus far issued by the commission.

The Consumers Union of the United States, responding to a request by the Consumer Product Safety Commission, has developed a safety standard for power lawn mowers and prepared an economic analysis of that standard.[1] An alternative economic analysis of the Consumers Union standard was prepared by the Stanford Research Institute (SRI) for the Outdoor Power Equipment Institute (OPEI), which represents the lawn mower industry. CPSC was scheduled to announce in early 1976 its decision on whether the standard developed by the Consumers Union would be promulgated. Once promulgated, the standard would be binding on all power lawn mowers manufactured after the effective date. These comments provide an evaluation of the economic analysis and the standard proposed by the

This chapter is edited from "Proposed Lawn Mower Safety Standard," Comments of the Council on Wage and Price Stability before the Consumer Product Safety Commission, October 14, 1975.

[1] In July 1974, the Consumer Product Safety Commission invited parties to submit proposed standards for lawn mower safety (see 39 Fed. Reg. 26662). A bid to develop and submit such a standard was subsequently made by Consumers Union of the United States and accepted by CPSC (see 39 Fed Reg. 37803).

Consumers Union. The study draws on the analyses of both Consumers Union and SRI.

The evidence shows that the proposed lawn mower safety standard will impose substantial costs on consumers in the form of higher lawn mower prices. The standard is comprehensive and, consequently, expensive. For example, Consumers Union's figures imply that the average price of walk-behind mowers will increase 32 percent and the average price of riding mowers will increase 13 percent. SRI estimates that walk-behind mowers will increase between 30 and 74 percent in price, while riding mowers will increase between 19 and 30 percent, depending on which alternatives in the standard are finally chosen. Furthermore, the largest percentage increase will be at the lower end of the lawn mower price range and will likely be borne by those individuals least able to afford them. Additional costs will be borne by producers, both because of compliance with the standard and because of lost sales. Since the impact of the proposed standard on costs is substantial, it is important that the proposal be supported by a sound, objective analysis of the purported benefits.

In general, the objective of public policy with respect to product safety should be to minimize all accident-related costs. This includes the direct costs of accidents themselves and the costs of reducing the occurrence of accidents. As more stringent standards are imposed, direct accident costs tend to fall while the additional costs of accident prevention rise. If the decline in costs associated with accidents is larger than the rise in costs associated with the more stringent standard—that is, if the incremental benefits of the regulation exceed the incremental costs—then the new standard is considered to be an improvement.

In terms of cost-benefit analysis, a calculation of accident costs includes all the tangible and intangible costs arising out of injuries caused by lawn mowers. The benefits of the safety standard would be the amount by which the accident costs are reduced as a result of having safer mowers. Accident prevention costs are reflected in the increased price of a safe mower (one complying with the standard); they should also include the costs borne by those individuals who choose not to purchase the more expensive, safer product but would have purchased the less expensive product were it available. These prevention costs are the costs of the standard. Thus, for the lawn mower safety standard to be justifiable, the costs of the standard should be smaller than the benefits.

It is the conclusion of this study, after a review of available evidence, that the lawn mower standard proposed by the Consumers Union should not be implemented. The evidence, even as presented and interpreted by Consumers Union, suggests that the benefits of the standard are not sufficient to justify the considerable costs imposed on lawn mower consumers as a result of the standard.

The analysis prepared by Consumers Union has serious weaknesses. First, the softness of the underlying data and the arbitrary assumptions that are made at several key points in the analysis provide a weak basis for making a decision on the standard. The benefits of the standard are obtained by first estimating the costs of lawn mower injuries and then estimating the effectiveness of the standard in reducing those costs. But the information available on lawn mower injuries—the basis for these estimates—is not very solid. In addition, the Consumers Union study provides no support for the most important estimate in the report, the estimate that the standard will result in a 75 percent reduction in lawn mower injuries. Second, even if the data and assumptions of Consumers Union were accepted, the standard still does not pass a cost-benefit test. That is to say, even by Consumers Union's own estimate, benefits are smaller than costs.

Because of the large impact on consumers, CPSC should obtain more reliable information on the nature and incidence of lawn mower injuries and on the effectiveness of the proposed standard before proceeding further. The commission should first rank the various components of the proposed standard in terms of their possible cost-effectiveness. These components should then be more thoroughly reviewed and analyzed. Only those components that can be shown to have benefits larger than costs should be implemented.

The following discussion concentrates on the cost-benefit analysis of Consumers Union, because they are the authors of the standard, and only briefly summarizes the SRI study. The estimates of costs and benefits of the proposed standard are discussed, and these estimates are used to compute cost-benefit ratios. As will be explained more fully below, this study reaches the conclusion that both Consumers Union and SRI computed their cost-benefit ratios incorrectly.

The Costs of Lawn Mower Injuries

As both Consumers Union and SRI stress throughout their reports, the available data on the costs of lawn mower injuries are very soft. In many cases, Consumers Union uses low, medium, and high estimates for particular costs so that a range of estimates is presented. In estimating the costs, Consumers Union has frequently made arbitrary judgments, and they have pointed out some of these. In some cases, the manner in which the estimates are made is not clearly explained, so that these estimates also appear to be arbitrary. Examples of these are given below. Although satisfactory explanations may exist, they are not given in the report. Furthermore, a surprisingly large weight is placed on the relatively intangible costs of pain and suffering associated with injuries. These costs are estimated to account for more than half of the total costs; this does not seem reasonable without further justification.

The analysis presents estimates for the costs of four categories of injuries: (1) nonfatal injuries treated in the emergency room of a hospital, (2) injuries treated in a physician's office, (3) eye injuries not included in (1), and (4) deaths. Total numbers of these injuries are estimated and are classified according to both type of injury and seven hazard areas of lawn mower operation—blade contact, thrown objects, steering and stability, brakes and drive train, electric shock, fire and burns, and noise. The standard concentrates on minimizing the likelihood of injuries in these seven areas. The costs of the injuries are then estimated and allocated to the seven areas.

Consumers Union's cost figures were obtained through the following sequence of estimates:

- Estimates of the total number of injuries in each of the four injury categories

- Estimates of the severity and types of injuries within the first two categories

- Allocation among the hazard areas of the lawn mower

- Estimates of the costs of each type of injury.

Consumers Union concluded, on the basis of their estimates, that annual accident costs, excluding the costs of pain and suffering, range between $47,771,000 and $412,656,000, with a medium estimate of $110,076,100. When pain and suffering costs are included, the range is $111,194,200 to $775,185,800, with a medium estimate of $233,607,800. These estimates illustrate the striking characteristics of the report, which are the wide range of most estimates and the large value placed on nonquantifiable pain and suffering costs. In this case, pain and suffering accounts for more than half of the low and medium cost estimates and almost half of the high estimate.

Number of Injuries. The number of injuries related to lawn mowers, which is the basis of estimates of the benefits of the standard, is not known with any degree of accuracy. For example, a survey by Market Facts, Inc., estimates a total of 190,000 injuries annually but notes that a range of plus or minus 100 percent is needed to achieve a 95 percent level of confidence.

Consumers Union uses an estimate of 58,500 for lawn mower injuries requiring emergency hospital care and estimates a range of 44,000 to 73,000 for a 95 percent level of confidence. The source for these estimates appears to be data from CPSC's National Electronic Injury Surveillance System (NEISS).

The number used for injuries treated in physicians' offices is 100,000. Support for this figure comes from a 1957 Georgia study and from National Safety Council data that show a total of 150,000 lawn mower injuries annually. Of course, the relevance of an eighteen-year-old study to a product like the power lawn mower is questionable.

It is estimated that 1,000 injuries involving loss of an eye, many of which bypass hospital emergency rooms, occur annually. The source for this appears to be a survey of 300 opthalmologists. Finally, it is estimated that 30 deaths occur annually because of lawn mowers. This figure receives some support from death certificates and NEISS data. Clearly, there is a definite need for more reliable information on the nature and numbers of lawn mower injuries.

Distribution of Injuries. The total number of various types of injuries requiring emergency hospital care is obtained by extrapolating from the NEISS data. The NEISS data are broken down into type of injury (burn, amputation, laceration, and so forth) and the proportion of injuries of each type requiring hospitalization. These data are then factored up to the national level of 58,500 injuries.

Consumers Union states that very little is known about the severity of injuries treated in physicians' offices, but they assume that these injuries are less severe than those treated in hospital emergency rooms.

Allocation to Hazard Areas. The numbers and costs of injuries are distributed among the seven hazard areas so that the standard can be evaluated. No explanation is given about how the distribution is made. Yet, this step is most important in the analysis because it provides the basis for computing cost-benefit ratios for different parts of the standard. This lack of an explanation is a severe defect in Consumers Union's analysis.

Costs. For nonfatal injuries reported in the NEISS survey of hospital emergency rooms, costs are calculated for each category of injury by adding the medical costs; the costs of being incapacitated from work, school, and housework; and the costs of permanent disability. The medical expenses have been estimated by a physician with extensive experience in treating lawn mower injuries.

The cost of a day incapacitated is assumed to be $40. This is then multiplied by low, medium, and high estimates for days incapacitated for each type of injury and according to whether the injury requires hospitalization. For example, the low, medium, and high estimates for a leg laceration requiring hospitalization are two, eight, and thirty days incapacitated at a cost of $80, $320, and $1,200.

The costs of permanent disability are calculated by taking the number of weeks allowed by the Federal Employees' Compensation Act and multiplying this figure by two-thirds of the assumed average wage rate of $225 per week. This is the medium estimate. Low and high estimates are obtained by multiplying the medium estimate by one-half and five, respectively. The justification for this procedure is not given; therefore it seems rather arbitrary.

The total of these quantifiable accident costs is $71,676,100, with a range of $28,821,200 to $259,686,000. In support of these estimates, Consumers Union states that the high figure is close to amounts reported from legal settlements. It is questioned, however, whether legal settlements reflect costs or speculations about what a jury might award. (Recent problems concerning medical malpractice settlements suggest that jury awards may sometimes exceed what might reasonably be considered as just compensation for damages.)

To these figures a dollar amount for pain and suffering is added. This is computed by multiplying the medium dollar cost estimate for days incapacitated by low, medium, and high factors. For example, the factors for a leg laceration requiring hospitalization are two, four, and ten. Since the medium cost estimate for days incapacitated for this type of injury is $320, the low, medium, and high estimates of the costs of pain and suffering are $640, $1,280, and $3,200. As Consumers Union admits in its report, this procedure is arbitrary.

When the costs of pain and suffering are included, the costs of nonfatal injuries treated in the emergency room of a hospital are $173,117,800, with a range of $81,094,200 to $494,135,800. Clearly, a tremendous weight is placed on pain and suffering. These costs account for more than half of the medium estimate of costs.

Consumers Union states that its estimates of injuries treated in physicians' offices have been done very conservatively. As was noted above, little is known about the characteristics of injuries treated in physicians' offices. Consumers Union estimates a range of $6,200,000 to $27,000,000, with a medium figure of $11,400,000 excluding pain and suffering. Including pain and suffering, the estimate is $27,400,000 with a range of $14,200,000 to $127,000,000.

Eye injuries (permanent loss of vision) are estimated to cost $24,000,000 with a range of $12,000,000 to $120,000,000, excluding pain and suffering and $25,590,000 with a range of $12,900,000 to $124,050,000 including pain and suffering. For some reason, pain and suffering are not very costly here.

The separate estimate for eye injuries is provided because ophthalmologists bypass the emergency room, and the NEISS figures underestimate the total. This may also happen with other types of injuries, though no estimate is provided.

The estimate for the costs of deaths (which can of course be quantified only by making arbitrary assumptions for purposes of analysis) is $3,000,000 with a range of $750,000 to $6,000,000 excluding pain and suffering, and $7,500,000 with a range of $3,000,000 to $30,000,000 including pain and suffering. Even though the highest outside estimate of the cost of a death cited in the report is $240,000 (by the National Highway Traffic Safety Administration), this figure is used as a *medium* estimate and a high estimate of $1,000,000 is used.

The total costs for all categories are $110,076,100 with a range of $47,771,200 to $412,656,000 excluding pain and suffering, and $233,607,800 with a range of $111,194,200 to $755,185,800 including pain and suffering.

It is difficult to estimate the likelihood of accidents with different types of lawn mowers because 70 percent of the injuries in the NEISS data are not specified according to lawn mower type. Furthermore, data on the numbers of each type of lawn mower are limited, and no data on intensity of use are available. Nonetheless, the report includes some discussion of the causes of injuries in each of the hazard areas. This discussion is based on observations that were not drawn randomly and hence the information conveyed is of limited use. Also, the NEISS data show injuries *associated with* various products but not necessarily *caused by* these products.

The Standard's Effect on Lawn Mower Prices

The lawn mower standard is a performance standard rather than a design standard, and thus the costs of implementing it will depend on the manufacturers' engineering ingenuity. Consumers Union has estimated the cost increases imposed by the standard from responses to a questionnaire sent to manufacturers. There is some reason to suspect that the manufacturers' estimates may be high.

According to the Consumers Union's own estimates, the proposed standard would add $40, or 32 percent, to the price of walk-behind mowers (the average price is now $125) and would add $112, or 13 percent, to the price of riding mowers and garden tractors (the average price is now $850). Consumers Union's estimates contrast sharply with SRI's estimates of a 30 to 74 percent increase in the price of walk-behind mowers and a 19 to 30 percent increase in the price of riding mowers, depending on the final form of the standard. According to both estimates, the less expensive walk-behind mowers will increase proportionately more in price than the more expensive riding mowers.

The total annual cost, assuming no loss of sales, is estimated to be $383,490,000. If unit sales decline by 30 percent, as the Outdoor Power Equipment Institute estimates, the total cost is stated to be $268,443,000. Since the lawn mower industry is a large industry with sales of $1.2 billion in 1974, the potential economic impact is not insignificant. Thus, the estimates of the impact on sales deserve closer scrutiny and OPEI's estimate should be carefully reviewed. Furthermore, Consumers Union's reasoning, which appears to argue that a decline in sales will increase the net social benefits of the standard, is disturbing. When sales decline, consumers are losing the benefits of the product. The implication of the Consumers Union's report is that a decline in sales would reduce the annual cost and improve the cost-benefit picture. That is, the cost figure would be reduced while the benefit figure stayed the same, thus decreasing the cost-benefit ratio. Clearly, this implication is not correct. A very expensive safety standard that induces consumers to decrease substantially their purchases will impose costs that are not included in the cost figure.[2]

Finally, using the information supplied by the manufacturers, Consumers Union distributes the costs among the seven hazard areas in order to make comparisons with the benefits.

---

[2] A measure of the additional cost is the loss in consumer's surplus. Consumer's surplus, roughly speaking, is the difference between what individuals are willing to pay for a product and what they actually pay. That is to say, it is a measure of the value attributed to a product in addition to its cost. When the price of a product rises, there is a loss of consumer's surplus. Under certain assumptions, this can be approximated by one-half the difference between the two cost figures (for the different levels of sales). The total cost, if sales decline by 30 percent, including the loss in consumer's surplus, is then $325,966,500. To avoid confusion, the figures of Consumers Union will still be used.

Cost-Benefit Comparisons

As stated at the outset, the purpose of a safety standard is to reduce injuries and the costs associated with them. Clearly, with respect to the lawn mower safety standard, much more review is needed on this critical subject. Consumers Union estimates that the standard will reduce injuries and injury costs by 75 percent, though this reduction is not distributed evenly across the hazard areas. No explanation is given for this estimate and it seems highly arbitrary. SRI estimates a 50 percent reduction in injury costs. They make some attempt to support this figure, though they suggest that no accurate prediction is possible. Yet, this figure is perhaps the most important single estimate in the analysis. The lack of support for this figure makes the entire analysis suspect because this number multiplied by the injury cost figures discussed above provides the benefit figure used in calculating the cost-benefit ratios.

Much of the reduction in accident costs will not accrue directly to consumers because they are already insured against many of these costs. For example, many consumers carry health insurance and would not be paying for the bulk of their medical expenses. If an individual can take sick leave with pay from his job, then implicitly he is insured against the loss in pay resulting from injury. Furthermore, it is doubtful whether the lawn mower standard would result in a decline in insurance costs because lawn mower accidents are a small portion of total injuries and illnesses.[3]

In the report, a comparison of costs and benefits is made according to each hazard area and according to lawn mower type. Since the distribution of injury costs to hazard areas has not been explained, however, and since the report states that information on the relationship between injuries and lawn mower type is limited, the meaning of these figures is questionable. This information is needed to determine which portions of the standard are most worthwhile.

Overall cost-benefit ratios are presented for medium and high estimates of injury costs including and excluding pain and suffering.[4] A sales level equal to 1973–1974 is assumed as well as a 30 percent reduction in sales. For the sales level equal to 1973–1974 when pain

---

[3] In a perfectly functioning market, any reduction in the probability of injury should be translated into lower insurance rates. Since it is assumed that insurance rates will not decline as a result of the lawn mower standard, and since consumers are partially insured, the benefits of the standard will be divided between consumers and insurance companies.

[4] Although it is more usual to compute benefit-cost ratios, the Consumers Union report refers to cost-benefit ratios, and that convention is followed here.

and suffering costs are excluded, the cost-benefit ratio using the medium injury cost estimate is 4.6 (that is, costs are 4.6 times as high as benefits) and the ratio using the high injury cost estimate is 1.2. When pain and suffering are included, the cost-benefit ratio using the medium injury cost estimate is 2.2 and the ratio using the high cost estimate is 0.7. For the 30 percent reduction in sales excluding pain and suffering, the cost-benefit ratios using the medium and high injury cost estimates are, respectively, 3.2 and 0.9. Including pain and suffering, these ratios are 1.5 and 0.5.

Thus, by Consumers Union's medium cost estimates, which can be assumed to represent their best guesses, the costs of the standard are larger than the benefits. As is shown below, however, Consumers Union's cost-benefit ratios are too low because they use an incorrect method to compute the ratios.

The Correct Way to Compute the Cost-Benefit Ratio. Consumers Union has taken the increment in cost for one year's lawn mower sales and compared this figure with the total benefits, assuming the entire lawn mower stock conforms with the safety standard. They state that this procedure is valid because they are considering the first year in which all the mowers conform with the standard. This is not valid, however, because the increased cost would be borne at the time of purchase whereas the benefits would be spread out over the subsequent years of the lawn mower's life. Put differently, Consumers Union has assumed that all the benefits would occur simultaneously with the costs. This underestimates the ratio of costs to benefits—that is, it overestimates the ratio of benefits to costs.

This can be shown by some examples using the Consumers Union data. SRI estimates that there are 40 million lawn mowers. Consumers Union estimates that 7.6 million lawn mowers were sold during 1973–1974; the SRI report gives a similar number. If this is the general pattern, then approximately one-fifth of the mowers are replaced each year and the average life of a mower is five years. The medium estimate of benefits including pain and suffering is $175,207,000 for the entire lawn mower stock for a year. Dividing that number by five gives the annual benefits for one year's volume ($35,041,000). If this saving is constant over the lawn mower's life, the discounted stream of benefits over the five years (assuming a 10 percent discount rate) is $132,840,000.[5] Using the cost figure pro-

---

[5] This example is for illustrative purposes. This figure can be recomputed using whatever discount rate is thought to be appropriate.

vided for one year's sales ($383,489,000), the cost-benefit ratio is 2.89. The figure reported by Consumers Union is 2.2.

If sales are reduced by 30 percent, this means that approximately 5 million mowers will be sold each year. If the total lawn mower stock remains 40 million (which is probably unrealistic, though there is no basis for using a different figure), this means that approximately one-eighth of the stock will be replaced each year and that the average lawn mower will last eight years. The annual benefits are then $21,901,000 ($175,207,000 divided by eight). The discounted stream of benefits over the eight years (at a 10 percent discount rate) is $116,842,000. The costs for the 30 percent reduction in sales are $268,500,000. The cost-benefit ratio is thus 2.3, as compared with 1.5 reported by Consumers Union.

It is rather misleading to suggest that the cost-benefit ratios are more favorable when sales are reduced. Some serious costs are being ignored. Clearly, some people will not buy mowers as frequently at the higher prices. Those consumers who would have purchased the cheaper, more hazardous mower bear a cost that is not reflected in the cost figures being used.

An extreme example illustrates this point. If the standard were so expensive that lawn mower sales dropped to zero, according to the reasoning of Consumers Union, the standard would be costless. This is clearly absurd. There will be a substantial cost to all those who would have purchased lawn mowers in the absence of the standard. Furthermore, if sales decline, the more hazardous mowers will be replaced more slowly. All mowers, including those conforming to the standard, may become more hazardous with age. If, for example, the higher prices associated with the new standard induce people to replace their mowers every eight years rather than every five years, there may be a higher incidence of injury associated with product failures. This may be the case especially with the more complicated machinery required by the standard.

Disaggregated Cost-Benefit Ratios. It is instructive to look behind the aggregate cost-benefit ratios to the ratios that are disaggregated according to hazard areas. When the medium estimate of cost including pain and suffering is used, three out of seven portions of the standard, including the two most expensive (blade contact, brakes and drive train), have cost-benefit ratios greater than 1. Together these account for 81 percent of the cost of the standard. In particular, the portion of the standard dealing with blade contact would cost $252,958,000 (assuming the 1973–1974 sales level), which is 66 percent of the total cost of the standard. This blade contact provision, clearly the most expensive, has a cost-benefit ratio of 2.42—that is, the costs of this provision are 2.42 times as large as the benefits provided in terms of injury reductions. Only those portions of the standard dealing with thrown objects, steering and stability, and electric shock have cost-benefit ratios smaller than 1—that is, their benefits exceed their costs. These are among the cheapest portions of the standard. No cost-benefit ratio is given for noise because no benefits are estimated. It should be noted that these are the cost-benefit ratios provided by Consumers Union, which are likely to be underestimates of the actual cost-benefit ratios.

SRI's Analysis

Stanford Research Institute has also done a cost-benefit analysis on the proposed standard, and their results are summarized here. They estimate that the annual costs of lawn mower injuries are approximately $400 million, which is higher than Consumers Union's medium estimate including pain and suffering. SRI estimates that the incremental cost to the consumer of complying with the standard is $520 million, which is also higher than Consumers Union's estimate, for a market of approximately 5 million units (one-eighth of the stock). They estimate that the standard will be 50 percent effective, yielding a yearly savings in accident costs of $25 million (0.5 times $400 million divided by eight). Using this data and following the method of computing a cost-benefit ratio described above, one arrives at a ratio of 3.9 over the eight-year time span. (SRI has also computed their cost-benefit ratio incorrectly and does not arrive at the figure reported here.)

The Effect on Competition

A wide-ranging standard such as the one proposed is likely to impose substantial costs that smaller firms would be unable to absorb. SRI estimates that, out of sixty to seventy-five lawn mower suppliers currently operating, only thirty-five to fifty will be left in five years. Although this may not have a significant effect on the competitiveness of the industry, the costs to the small businessman should be considered.

Concluding Comments

On the basis of the medium estimates including the costs of pain and suffering, the proposed standard has costs larger than its benefits, as estimated by Consumers Union. The standards for blade contact, brakes and drive train, and fire and burns—which together account for 81 percent of the cost—all have cost-benefit ratios larger than 1. The noise standard has no quantifiable benefits.

The cost-benefit picture becomes more favorable only when the high injury cost estimates combined with high cost estimates for pain and suffering are used. It is doubtful, however, that these estimates are reasonable.

The assumptions used in the analysis and the softness of the data have been criticized in this study. The number of lawn mower injuries is not really known with precision; the costs of pain and suffering are estimated in a highly arbitrary manner and seem very large; and the assumption that the standard would be 75 percent effective, a key assumption in the analysis, is not supported. On the latter point, SRI thinks that the standard would be only 50 percent effective.

It has been assumed here that the medium estimates reflect Consumers Union's best guesses. On the basis of those estimates, the standard as it now stands should not be implemented. Consumers Union argues (only very tentatively, to be sure) that the cost-benefit ratio does not have to be smaller than 1 because consumers may be averse to the injury risks connected with present lawn mowers. This is a weak argument. There is no compelling evidence that consumers are risk averse at the margin. As has been mentioned, consumers are already insured against many of the potential costs of accidents; they are already substantially protected against the risks. If Consumers Union believes their argument is valid, they should present some evidence for it. It is not sufficient, after deriving detailed estimates of costs and benefits, to brush these estimates aside by saying they do not mean anything because consumers may be risk averse.

In conclusion, the economic analysis prepared by Consumers Union, as it now stands, does not provide a sound basis for making a decision on a standard that will impose such large costs on consumers. Further work should be done in this area and more reliable estimates should be obtained. CPSC should proceed by ranking segments of the proposed standard in terms of their possible cost-effectiveness. These segments should then be more thoroughly reviewed and analyzed. Only those segments that can be shown to have benefits larger than costs should be implemented.

To obtain more reliable estimates of cost-effectiveness, better information is needed on the incidence of lawn mower injuries and, especially, on the effectiveness of individual segments of the standard in preventing these injuries. Perhaps a sample of lawn mower users would provide more reliable information on injuries. Information might be obtained by looking at the experience with existing lawn mowers; substantial variation may have occurred already in their safety characteristics. An experimental approach might be useful, under which lawn mowers conforming to a safety standard might be manufactured on a small scale and their safety record monitored. All these suggestions require additional expenditures by CPSC, a factor that should be taken into account. In any case, some additional expenditure will be necessary in order to make an informed decision.

Once better information and more reliable estimates are obtained, they should be taken into account in formulating a standard. Above all, however, the standard should not impose costs that are larger than the benefits it provides.

The CPSC formally proposed a comprehensive lawn mower standard on May 5, 1977.[6] The proposal contains a "dead-man control" provision, which is a slight modification of the provision proposed by Consumers Union. In addition, the CPSC dropped requirements relating to noise control because of steps being taken by the Environmental Protection Agency to issue noise standards for lawn mowers.

The Council on Wage and Price Stability submitted comments to the CPSC on its proposal on August 15, 1977. According to new CPSC and SRI analyses, the costs of the standard would outweigh its benefits. The council was critical of both studies for not considering the impact of a voluntary safety standard, with which a substantial number of mowers have complied in recent years.

A final standard has not yet been promulgated.

---

[6] 42 Fed. Reg. 23052 (May 5, 1977).

6

Matchbook Safety

Milton Z. Kafoglis

The purpose of the Consumer Product Safety Act is to protect the public against excessive risks of injury associated with consumer products. The commission, however, has had great difficulty determining which products to tackle first. Swimming pool slides and matchbooks, which preoccupied the agency during its first years, seemed poor selections for a new agency that had a broad mandate to be a "no nonsense," tough regulator in a world made increasingly hazardous by a plethora of unsafe consumer products. Some critics of consumer product regulation have asserted that the selection of matchbooks and swimming pool slides simply proved that a federal agency had been created in response to a problem that did not exist. A more sympathetic view would focus on the lack of adequate data to develop a system of priorities and on the unusual "collegial" organization of the commission. The matchbook case reveals the serious data problem that exists and the tenuous nature of the causes of those injuries that can be tabulated—was it the product, the consumer, or the environment? The matchbook case is an example of what happens when an attempt is made to prevent injuries without really isolating and quantifying their causes.

The Consumer Product Safety Commission (CPSC) has proposed a safety standard for matchbooks that would require extensive changes in the ordinary paper matchbooks manufactured in the United States

This chapter is edited from "Proposed Matchbook Standards," Comments of the Council on Wage and Price Stability before the Consumer Product Safety Commission, June 1, 1976.

or imported into the country.[1] Under the proposed standard, match-books would have to conform to a variety of specifications, including:

- Improved quality control, such as certain performance standards and test procedures for fragmentation of matchheads, split matchheads, and delayed ignition

- Location of the friction, or striking surface, on the outside back cover near the bottom of the matchbook (reverse friction)

- A flame that would self-extinguish within one-half inch down from the top of the splint and within a fifteen-second burn time

- A latching device that would inhibit access by children.

A comprehensive analysis of the benefits and costs of the standards is not now available, and the technical feasibility of some of the standards is in question. The commission is required by section 9 of the Consumer Product Safety Act to take into account the probable effects of the standards on the utility, cost, and availability of match-books as well as on competition, manufacturing, and commercial practices.[2] A detailed study of the probable effects was prepared for the commission by Battelle Columbus Laboratories.

On the basis of the information available, the present study estimates that the proposed standard could raise costs to consumers by approximately $68 million annually, could diminish the utility of matches to their users, and could result in greater corporate concentration in the matchbook industry. The study also questions how effective the proposal would be in reducing match-related accidents; in some respects, the standard might lead to an increase in accidents. Thus, the study recommends that the CPSC make special efforts to develop and analyze additional data before promulgating the standard.

Risks Addressed by the Standard

The standard is intended to reduce unreasonable risks of death or serious injury to consumers or users of bookmatches and to "address adequately the primary hazard of matchbooks which is the risk of injury to children who play with or otherwise misuse bookmatches."[3] CPSC's analysis of the risk of injury is based primarily on data pro-

---

[1] 41 Fed. Reg. 14112 (April 1, 1976). The CPSC had commenced a proceeding for development of a safety standard for matchbooks on September 4, 1974 (see 39 Fed. Reg. 32050).

[2] 15 U.S.C. section 2058(c)(1).

[3] 41 Fed. Reg. 14112.

vided by the National Electronic Injury Surveillance System (NEISS), which collects data on injuries related to various products from a statistically selected sample of hospital emergency rooms. CPSC also conducts in-depth investigations of selected injuries associated with products.

On the basis of NEISS sample data, CPSC estimates that during fiscal year 1975 approximately 9,500 people throughout the United States were treated in hospital emergency rooms for injuries related to matches. This national estimate is based on a sample of 368 actual cases reported through the NEISS system. According to CPSC, serious burn injuries are sometimes treated in special hospital burn units that may not report to NEISS; the number of injuries may thus be underestimated. Injuries treated directly in physicians' offices also are not included in the estimate. On the other hand, the estimates include injuries associated with wooden matches and, to this extent, yield an overestimate of matchbook injuries.[4] Thus, there is no firm figure of the total number of injuries to which the proposed standard is addressed. The NEISS data that are available, however, combined with in-depth investigations made by CPSC, can provide some information concerning the types and probable causes of matchbook injuries.

Table 6–1 summarizes the age and disposition of the 368 victims of match-related injuries included in the NEISS sample. Slightly more than 97 percent of these victims who entered emergency rooms were treated and released; the remaining 3 percent required further treatment in the hospital. Thus, for fiscal year 1975, of the estimated 9,500 victims of match injuries, 285 could be described as having a serious enough injury to require hospitalization. Children less than five years of age, the primary group to which the standard is addressed, accounted for 703 of the victims (7.4 percent of the total); of these young victims, 57 (0.6 percent of the total) required hospital treatment beyond the emergency room.[5]

Though these data, which are the most reliable available, indicate that the vast majority of injuries are not severe, they do not necessar-

---

[4] Wooden matches account for 14.6 percent of total match shipments. See W.E. Riddle, *Analysis of the Book Match Industry and the Potential Impact of a Proposed Standard on Book Matches*, report to the Consumer Product Safety Commission (Columbus, Ohio: Battelle Columbus Laboratories, March 1975), p. 8; hereinafter referred to as Battelle Report. A more complete analysis is being prepared by Battelle.

[5] Children less than five years of age constitute 11 percent of the total population. See Elaine Tyrrell, *Preliminary Risk-of-Injury Report* (Consumer Product Safety Commission, October 1975), p. 5.

TABLE 6-1

DISPOSITION OF VICTIMS WITH MATCH-RELATED INJURIES IN NEISS SAMPLE BY AGE GROUP, FISCAL YEAR 1975

(number; percent of total in parentheses)

Age Group	Treated and Released			Treated and Transferred			Hospitalized			Total		
	Male	Female	Total	Male	Female	Total	Male	Female	Total	Male	Female	Total
Less than 5	17	8	25 (6.8)	1	0	1 (0.3)	1	0	1 (0.3)	19	8	27 (7.4)
5–9	11	6	17 (4.6)	2	0	2 (0.5)	0	1	1 (0.3)	13	7	20 (5.4)
10–19	44	35	79 (21.5)	0	0	0	1	0	1 (0.3)	45	35	80 (21.8)
20–44	86	99	185 (50.2)	0	0	0	1	0	1 (0.3)	87	99	186 (50.5)
45–64	23	23	46 (12.5)	0	0	0	2	1	1 (0.3)	25	24	49 (13.8)
65 and over	2	2	4 (1.1)	0	0	0	0	0	3 (0.8)	2	2	4 (1.1)
Total, age known	183	173	356 (96.7)	3	0	3 (0.8)	5	2	7 (2.0)	191	175	366 (99.5)
Total, age unknown	1	1	1	2 (0.5)	0	0	0	0	0	1	1	2 (0.5)
Grand total	184	174	357 (97.2)	3	0	5 (0.8)	5	2	7 (2.0)	192	176	368 (100.0)

SOURCE: Elaine A. Tyrrell, *Preliminary Risk-of-Injury Report* (Consumer Product Safety Commission, October 1975).

ily imply that these injuries are "reasonable" or that mandatory matchbook standards should not be imposed. The 409 in-depth investigations of selected injuries made by CPSC reveal instances of tragic injury and death. These in-depth investigations reveal the accident sequence in the more serious injury cases and can be useful in the design of standards.

Table 6–2 summarizes the NEISS match-related injuries by the part of the body affected. Of the 368 victims, 220 (59.5 percent of the total) sustained injuries to the eye. Such eye injuries are usually caused by fragmentation, sparking, and broken matchheads. The in-depth investigations reveal that almost all such injuries are sustained by adults and are in the "treated and released" category. Injuries to the hand and fingers (15.3 percent of the total) can be related to flaming matchbooks caused by fragmentation or poor design of the matchbook package; these injuries also are primarily in the "treated and released" category. In sum, injuries to the eye, hand, or fingers do not appear to be severe. They constitute about 75 percent of the injuries and can be related to fragmentation, poor design of the matchbook, or other match malfunction.

The remaining 25 percent of the injuries involved matches associated with another substance—typically, clothing or some combustible matter such as gasoline, natural gas, or other flammable liquid. These types of injuries are usually more serious and are caused either by malfunction of the match (fragmentation) or "misuse, abuse, or carelessness." The latter category includes matches dropped on clothing, bedding, or other combustible substances and "playing" with matches.

CPSC does not carefully relate each of the causes of matchbook injuries to the type and cost of the standards required. Reverse friction and improved quality control, however, would address the vast majority of cases associated with fragmentation and match malfunction. Reverse friction has been voluntarily accepted by the industry and is rapidly becoming standard industry practice. On the other hand, firms differ in the degree of quality control exercised in the production of matches.

To address the injuries associated with clothing and other flammable products, CPSC has proposed a time-burn standard that requires that the match extinguish after burning fifteen seconds or one-half an inch. Injuries associated with "play" are addressed by a requirement that the matchbook cover be latched so that it will be "child-resistant." These components of the matchbook standard, especially the latching device, are the most costly to introduce and

TABLE 6–2

Diagnosis of Match-Related Injuries in NEISS Sample by Body Part Affected, Fiscal Year 1975
(number; percent of total in parentheses)

Diagnosis	Eye	Head	Hand	Finger	Leg	Over 25 Percent of the Body	Other	Unknown	Total
Thermal burn	104 (28.2)	34 (9.2)	33 (9.0)	17 (4.6)	9 (2.5)	12 (3.2)	1 (0.3)	0	210 (57.0)
All other burns	19 (5.1)	7 (1.9)	4 (1.1)	1 (0.3)	3 (0.8)	4 (1.1)	0	1 (0.3)	39 (10.6)
Contusion/abrasion	70 (19.0)	1 (0.3)	0	0	0	0	0	0	71 (19.3)
Dermititis/conjunctivitis	15 (4.0)	1 (0.3)	0	0	0	0	0	0	16 (4.3)
Laceration/puncture	0	4 (1.1)	0	0	1 (0.3)	0	0	0	5 (1.4)
Embedded foreign body	12 (3.2)	6 (1.6)	0	0	0	0	1 (0.3)	0	19 (5.2)
Ingestion/poisoning	0	0	0	0	0	2 (0.5)	3 (0.8)	0	5 (1.3)
Other[a]	0	1 (0.3)	1 (0.3)	0	0	1 (0.3)	0	0	3 (0.9)
Total	220 (59.5)	54 (14.7)	38 (10.4)	18 (4.9)	13 (3.6)	19 (5.2)	5 (1.4)	1 (0.3)	368 (100.0)

Source: Tyrrell, *Preliminary Risk-of-Injury Report.*
[a] Includes unknown.

will reduce the utility of matchbooks to consumers. Neither the time-burn match nor the child-resistant cover has been tested by CPSC, and their effectiveness has been seriously questioned.

Costs of the Standard

CPSC has made no estimates of the costs of implementing the various components of the standards. Nor are there any published industry data relating to the current costs of producing matchbooks. A major reason is that the matchbook industry has operated for more than thirty years under a consent decree issued by the Department of Justice. This consent decree apparently forbids manufacturers from sharing financial data. As a result, there is no trade association, and firms are reluctant to reveal information in an industry that seems to have become keenly competitive.

It has been reported, however, that matchbooks currently cost less than one cent each to produce.[6] This figure compares with an average revenue per matchbook of 0.49 cents calculated from data provided to CPSC by Battelle Columbus Laboratories.[7] Since net profit margins in the industry are very low (about 3 percent of sales), average revenue per matchbook should closely approximate average cost per matchbook. The figure of 0.49 cents per matchbook includes revenues from sales of special reproduction matches, which cost more to produce and include a larger profit margin.[8] Average revenue per matchbook of resale advertising matches is about one-third of a cent per matchbook.[9] This figure, however, may be somewhat below average cost of production because match manufacturers receive some advertising revenues from firms using resale matches as an advertising medium. Matches may be purchased at large supermarkets in caddies of fifty books for as little as 25 cents a caddy or one-half cent a matchbook. In the absence of a calculation by CPSC and taking into account industry reports and average revenues per matchbook, it is estimated that the average production cost per matchbook is about one-half cent.

CPSC has not estimated the increased cost of complying with

---

[6] Wall Street Journal, April 2, 1976, p. 6.

[7] Battelle Report, p. 20.

[8] Special reproduction matches are purchased by advertisers for promotional purposes and are given free to the user.

[9] Calculated from the Battelle Report, p. 21. Resale advertising matches are given away by tobacco shops, drug stores, and other outlets. They contain advertising and are distributed by the match manufacturer under a contractual arrangement with an advertiser.

the proposed matchbook standards.[10] Most officials of matchbook companies have not provided much information beyond describing the impact on production costs as "disastrous." In conversations with staff members of the Council on Wage and Price Stability, however, some producers voiced greater concern about the potential loss of markets to inexpensive butane disposable lighters, which are currently making steady inroads into the matchbook market. Other officials indicated concern about the reduction in the use of matches as an advertising medium because of higher costs and "degradation" of the product. Producers also spoke about the impact of the standards on the speed of the production process. Matchbooks are produced at very high speeds in an assembly process that is capital-intensive. The addition of the child-resistant latching device might reduce significantly the speed of the assembly process, hence reducing productivity and increasing the cost of matches.

One match manufacturer estimated that the increased cost per case of matches would be $8.06, or 0.32 cents a matchbook. Assuming the cost of matchbooks rises by one-third of a cent per unit, the total increased cost to advertisers and consumers would approximate $68–70 million (assuming there was no reduction in sales volumes and all of the cost increase could be "passed through").[11] "Free" matches probably would not disappear because the matchbook is a good advertising device, but their availability clearly would be curtailed by an amount that cannot readily be determined. "Free" matchbooks, in other words, would not be so freely available. In addition, the current trend toward disposable lighters would accelerate, creating a new and possibly greater safety hazard. Special reproduction matches, to which the standards do not apply, might also make inroads into the match market. Moreover, there are the "real" costs to many consumers who will receive an "inferior" (from their point of view) product.

In view of the inadequacies of the data available and the controversy concerning the use of benefit-cost analysis in the areas of health and safety, this study will simply point out some implications of the proposed standard. CPSC has made no estimate of the effectiveness of the standard, but, if the standard is assumed to be perfectly effective, approximately 9,500 injuries would be eliminated at a cost

---

[10] Battelle Columbus Laboratories is now preparing an economic analysis that may provide some of the necessary cost information.

[11] To the extent that sales fell off, the direct cost would be less than $68 million, but there would be negative effects on employment in the industry and on consumers who shifted to substitutes.

of \$7,157 per injury (\$69 million ÷ 9,500 = \$7,157). If only that proportion (about 3 percent) of injuries that lead to hospitalization is considered, approximately 285 injuries will be eliminated at a cost of \$240,000 per injury involving hospitalization (\$68 million ÷ 285 = \$238,596.49). It does not seem possible, however, that the standard will be perfectly effective. If the standard were 50 percent effective, the above cost figures would be doubled; if it were 25 percent effective, they would be quadrupled.

It should be noted that the proposed standard has various components, each of which involves different costs and has a particular impact on injuries. That is, each component of the standard has a different benefit-cost relation, and the CPSC has provided no information concerning these relations. It seems likely, though, that the most costly component, the latching requirement, would be the least effective in reducing injury. The data now available do not make it certain that the proposed standard would maximize injury reduction per unit of resources utilized. In other words, the standard might not minimize the cost of reducing a given number of injuries. Whether or not benefit-cost analysis is accepted, the need for rational criteria in the establishment of priorities cannot be denied.

Impact on the Matchbook Industry

The analysis of the matchbook industry undertaken by Battelle Columbus Laboratories indicates that the proposed standard would have a dramatic impact on the matchbook industry, especially on the smaller firms.

In 1975, the matchbook industry contained eleven firms and accounted for sales of less than \$120 million. It is a small industry composed of small firms, most of which have annual sales of less than \$10 million. Battelle reports that in 1975 the top four firms accounted for 77 percent of total industry sales and 91 percent of the after-tax profits earned in the industry. The industry is highly concentrated with respect to sales and even more concentrated with respect to profits. Very low profits, especially among the smaller firms, have encouraged consolidation of firms and a reduction in the number of plants. Thus, the current trend is toward greater concentration and fewer firms. This trend will be accentuated by adoption of the proposed standard as smaller firms find it impossible to handle the increase in capital costs that will be imposed.

The before-tax profits of the industry have been estimated at slightly more than \$4.3 million, or an estimated before-tax return on investment of between 6 and 8 percent; the after-tax yield is between 3 and 4 percent. The majority of match manufacturers are subsidiaries of larger conglomerate-type firms, and such firms would view major capital expenditures in their match divisions with a great deal of skepticism. According to the preliminary Battelle report, "It would be difficult to conceive of a professional business manager recommending an investment that will yield only 2½ to 3⅓ percent when monies could be used at a far greater return in some other area of the enterprise." As for the smaller firms, "a major capital investment might be sufficient to cause these firms to exit from the industry." Battelle concludes that "any major capital expenditure should be viewed as a vehicle that would result in consolidation of the industry, and probably would result in the exit of at least half the existing manufacturers."[12]

Toward Adoption of a Standard

The major standards proposed by CPSC include quality control and testing, time-burn limitation, and a child-resistant matchbook.

Virtually all the matchbook manufacturers have some sort of quality control program. It is recognized within the industry, however, that some firms produce a "better" match of more uniform quality than other firms. Promulgation of this component of the standard would likely not impose large additional costs on most firms. Since most injuries are caused by fragmentation, broken matchheads, and other types of match malfunction, the adoption of a reasonable quality standard promises to yield substantial additional benefits. Though the CPSC proposal contains specific tests, it is silent about sample size, frequency of testing, and the like. Thus, no estimate of these costs can be made. According to Battelle, certain match manufacturers will have to store sizable quantities of match stems before assembly, creating not only a fire hazard but also a space problem for many of the smaller manufacturers. One manufacturer has suggested that routine testing be eliminated, but that CPSC approve and certify the manufacturing process. CPSC should examine alternative means for implementing programs of quality control and should adopt the alternative that promises to achieve the desired quality at the lowest cost.

The time-burn provision may reduce injuries associated with the ignition of clothing and other fabrics, though there is controversy within the industry about the effectiveness of this provision. Rapid

---

[12] Battelle Report, p. 9.

technical progress has been made toward the development of self-extinguishing matches, and prototypes are now available. The cost of implementing this component of the standard is not known, however, and the technology is not available to all firms. CPSC is urged to determine the cost of a time-burn provision and the extent to which such a provision would succeed in eliminating the ignition of clothing and other types of fabric—an issue that is far from settled.

The most costly component of the proposed standard is the requirement that the matchbook be designed to reduce the likelihood of young children's gaining access to matches. A matchbook with a latching cover has been designed, but its efficiency and consumer reaction have not been tested. Examination of the prototype suggests that many users will find the latching device awkward and frustrating and will either leave the matchbook open or tear off the cover, possibly increasing rather than decreasing matchbook hazards. It is not obvious that the latching device is childproof. Indeed, it could entice increased play by children who are attracted by the "puzzle."

The latching mechanism would reduce production speeds and would require new capital expenditures for all firms in order to provide new latch machines, modify existing assembly machinery, and add new assembly machinery to maintain output at previous levels. In an industry that is already contracting and in which yield on investment is low, it appears that only five or six of the largest firms might elect to incur the capital expenditures required; smaller firms would then either be absorbed by the few dominant firms or would simply cease operation. The already high concentration ratio that prevails in the industry would increase, and the keen competition that now exists could be diminished or disappear. For these reasons, the CPSC is urged to withhold promulgation of the latching component of the proposed standard until its effectiveness and cost have been evaluated more fully.

Summary

More information is needed before a well-informed decision can be made about the proposed matchbook safety standard. CPSC is urged to (1) improve its analyses of risk of injury and of costs, (2) evaluate each component of the standard in terms of either a benefit-cost analysis or a cost-effectiveness analysis, (3) consider the impact on the viability and competitiveness of the matchbook industry, and (4) assess the new hazards that might be imposed by adopting the proposed matchbook standard.

After considerable debate, hearings, and publicity, the CPSC eventually issued final matchbook standards on May 4, 1977.[13] *The latching device and the time-burn provisions, by far the most costly and probably the least beneficial of the proposals, were deleted. Quality control, performance standards, and testing procedures, the least costly and possibly the most beneficial components, were incorporated in the new standards.*

Even these limited standards were challenged, however in D. D. Beane *v.* CPSC. *The U.S. Circuit Court of Appeals announced its decision on March 31, 1978, and in a unanimous decision the court struck down the performance standards and all test procedures. The major component that survived was reverse friction, an improvement that had already been made by the largest manufacturers. A key element in the court's decision was the failure of CPSC to demonstrate a causal connection between injuries and standards. The court found that the benefits of the standard were both small and tenuous and probably not worth the costs. The court relied on arguments similar to those of the Council on Wage and Price Stability, but it was much more severe in evaluating the logic, analysis, and facts that the CPSC presented in support of the standards. The court's stern judgment in the "matchbook case" should encourage improved analyses of product safety regulatory proposals in the future.*

---

[13] 42 Fed. Reg. 22660 (May 4, 1977).

7

Crash Protection for Auto Occupants

Thomas D. Hopkins and Gerald G. Threadgill

Since passage of the National Traffic and Motor Vehicle Safety Act of 1966, a long series of controversial rule-making proceedings has produced increasingly demanding requirements to afford automobile passengers greater crash protection. These requirements have included seat belts, ignition interlock systems that prevent ignition unless seat belts are fastened (voided by the Congress in 1974), and now passive restraints that provide protection whether or not a passenger buckles a seat belt. The Council on Wage and Price Stability intervened several times in these varied proceedings in 1975, 1976, and 1977; this study is drawn from the council's 1976 intervention.

In June 1976, the secretary of transportation requested comments on proposed revisions to the safety standard regarding devices designed to protect occupants of automobiles in the event of a crash.[1] Most notable among the suggested revisions was a proposal to mandate passive restraints, particularly the air-cushion restraint system known as the "air bag."

In the *Federal Register* notice, the secretary identified several regulatory and legislative actions under consideration.[2] The five principal alternatives cited were:

- Continuation of the existing requirement[3]

This chapter is edited from "Occupant Crash Protection Highway Safety Programs Standards: 49 CFR Part 571, 23 CFR Part 1204," Supplemental Statement on Behalf of the Council on Wage and Price Stability before the Secretary of Transportation, August 3, 1976.

[1] 41 Fed. Reg. 24070 (June 14, 1976), regarding proposed revisions in Federal Motor Vehicle Safety Standard (FMVSS) 208.

[2] Ibid., pp. 24074–76.

[3] The present form of FMVSS 208 "requires manufacturers to provide occupant protection in vehicles by one of three systems: (1) a completely passive restraint

- Inducement of the states to adopt and enforce laws making the use of safety belts mandatory

- Continuation of the present standard while a federally sponsored field test of passive restraints is conducted

- Mandatory passive restraints, whereby all automobiles manufactured after a given date would be required to have passive restraints

- Mandatory passive restraint option, whereby manufacturers would be required to provide consumers with the option of passive restraints in some or all of their models.

The present study concludes that, although the air bag appears promising, more testing should be done before these devices are mandated for a significant portion of the auto fleet. This view reflects the considerable uncertainty surrounding the benefits of air bags. Until now, data on the benefits of air bags have been derived largely from laboratory experiments. Actual field testing has been very limited for large cars and negligible for small cars. Yet, significant costs would be imposed on automobile purchasers if air bags were mandated. With such uncertainty regarding the expected benefits, it is possible that a regulation mandating passive restraint systems could well be inflationary.

Thus, this study makes two principal recommendations:

- Additional efforts should be made to increase the use of lap and shoulder belts.

- Air bags should be field tested in 100,000 vehicles (primarily small cars) before a decision is made about whether they should be mandated.

Evaluation of DOT's Economic Analysis

The U.S. Department of Transportation (DOT) prepared a benefit-cost analysis of the alternative crash protection systems, making use of four studies by the National Highway Traffic Safety Administra-

---

system providing protection in frontal, lateral, and roll-over crashes, or (2) a passive restraint system providing protection in frontal crashes combined with lap seat belts providing protection in lateral and roll-over crashes, or (3) lap and shoulder seat belts at the front outboard positions and lap seat belts for all other positions." A passive restraint system is defined as "a system that affords crash protection without requiring action on the part of the vehicle's occupant" (ibid., p. 24070, n. 2).

tion (NHTSA).[4] With minor exceptions, these analyses are extremely well done. Their methodology seems to be generally correct, and they are comprehensive both in their scope and in their use of currently available data. Although the studies do not provide the secretary of transportation with a clear-cut "best" alternative, they do provide good comparisons of alternatives under a number of assumed conditions.

In evaluating the cost of alternatives, DOT has made a solid attempt to determine lifetime costs. Indeed, DOT has reported carefully the discrepancies between NHTSA's cost estimates and those made by other parties. As the DOT evaluation notes, these discrepancies should be resolved before any final rule-making decision.

One important element of cost, however, was not adequately addressed by DOT's analysis. Specifically, the "inconvenience costs" incurred by the individual using any of the restraint systems should receive some treatment. The department's reluctance to address this issue is understandable, because such costs are virtually impossible to quantify with accuracy. Nevertheless, it should be made clear in the analysis that such costs do exist and that in some circumstances they must be substantial. In the extreme, such costs may explain why most motorists ignore widely distributed information on the effectiveness of lap and shoulder belts and fail to "buckle up." The inclusion of some measure of these costs could have a definite effect on the relative attractiveness of the alternatives and could help focus more attention on the importance of improving belt design.

Substantial disagreement appears to exist over some of the assumptions made by DOT in analyzing benefits. While it is conceded that net social benefits could result from improved passenger safety, not all would agree with DOT's method for estimating the benefits.

Certain questions arise regarding the statistics used in the studies to describe the effectiveness of different systems. DOT's analysts have been forced to rely on laboratory data as opposed to field test data. Since DOT lacked sufficient experience-based data, it has attempted to simulate that data by reporting a number of best, worst, and expected situations. These extrapolations could be improved if they were expanded to include different levels of utiliza-

---

[4] 41 Fed. Reg. 24078 as revised at 41 Fed. Reg. 31860; Conrad Cooke, *Passenger Car Occupant Injuries and Their Economic Impact* (National Highway Traffic Safety Administration, July 1976); William Boehly, *Effectiveness Levels of Various Occupant Restraint Systems* (NHTSA, July 1976); Conrad Cooke, *Usage of Occupant Crash Protection System* (NHTSA, July 1976); and Conrad Cooke, *Consumer Cost of Occupant Crash Protection Systems* (NHTSA, July 1976).

tion of lap belts in the air bag–lap belt system and different assumed levels of system defeat in the passive belt system.

DOT might improve its analysis of alternatives, but its treatment of benefit-cost ratios contains an even more serious flaw. The department has mistakenly used benefit-cost ratios to rank alternatives.[5] The original *Federal Register* notice correctly points out that "consideration of the total benefits and costs of a proposal are at least as important as their ratios."[6] DOT's benefit-cost analysis, however, states that "forming the ratio of the incremental benefits and costs gives an indication of the relative merits of the different objectives."[7] What is relevant for purposes of choosing among alternatives is not only the benefit-cost ratios but the extent to which social benefits *exceed* social costs.[8]

To illustrate the problem, Table 7–1 arrays DOT's cost and benefit data so as to show net social benefits.[9] Although the table does not define a specific solution, it does show the potential net gains associated with the alternative systems.

Comments on the Alternative Proposals

The following observations are offered with respect to the alternatives proposed by the secretary of transportation.

Utilization of Lap and Shoulder Belts. Data contained in DOT's economic analysis indicate that lap and shoulder belts, when worn, are effective in reducing death and injury in automobile accidents. Indeed, there would probably be no need for a public debate about the alternative proposals if the consuming public would wear the belts currently provided. As is quite evident, however, the majority of the public does not wear belts on a regular basis. Thus, a cost-

---

[5] 41 Fed. Reg. 31862.

[6] Ibid., p. 24073.

[7] Ibid., pp. 24079 and 31862.

[8] This is not to belittle the use of benefit-cost ratios. From an efficiency standpoint, a project should not be undertaken unless the benefit-cost ratio exceeds unity (that is, benefits exceed costs). Also, a properly drawn efficient proposal will have, to the degree feasible, a *marginal* benefit-cost ratio equal to unity (that is, the extra benefits from a slight "strengthening" of the standard are equal to the additional costs). Benefit-cost ratios of alternative (mutually exclusive) programs do not, however, reveal the quantitative differences between benefits and costs, and these are the relevant data for choosing among the alternatives.

[9] It should be kept in mind that the figures in Table 7-1 do not include the "inconvenience costs" experienced by the occupant in actuating the device (for example, buckling a lap belt).

TABLE 7–1

NET BENEFITS OF OCCUPANT CRASH PROTECTION SYSTEMS USING VARIOUS COST ESTIMATES

(millions of dollars)

Occupant Restraint System[a]	Net Benefits		
	Low cost estimates	NHTSA cost estimates	High cost estimates
Lap and shoulder (15%) and lap (5%) belt	679	579	479
Lap and shoulder (35%) and lap (5%) belt	1,975	1,875	1,775
Lap and shoulder belt (70%)	4,037	3,937	3,837
Lap and shoulder belt (100%)	5,981	5,881	5,781
Lap belt (100%)	—	3,760	—
Driver-only air cushion	—	2,404	1,504
Full front air cushion	3,383	2,483	883
Passive belts	—	3,320	—
Mandatory option			
5% air cushion	—	579	—
10% air cushion	—	579	—
25% air cushion	—	580	—

Dash (—): Not applicable.

[a] Percent in parentheses indicates assumed percent usage by occupants.

SOURCES: 41 Fed. Reg. 31863, Tables 2 and 3; and William Boehly, *Effectiveness Levels of Various Occupant Restraint Systems* (U.S. Department of Transportation, National Highway Traffic Safety Administration, July 1976).

effective solution to the issue may lie in efforts to attain a greater acceptance of nonpassive belt systems.

There are three separate areas in which resources might be employed to attain increased use of belts. First, a mandatory seat belt law as proposed by the secretary of transportation might be more cost-beneficial than any other alternative. Along these lines, it is unfortunate that data from required seat belt "experiments" in other countries are not available at the present time. DOT could, however, encourage one or more representative states to adopt a mandatory seat belt law, and this experience could provide useful data for a decision about a national mandatory belt law.

Second, a hard-line federally sponsored advertising program might increase the use of seat belts. Although advertising of the virtues of seat belts has been undertaken by NHTSA in the past with only limited success, it seems possible that a program directed to counteract currently held misconceptions about the use of belts might be effective. For example, the province of Ontario, Canada, has enjoyed some success with such a program.

Third, improving the belt systems themselves might be considered. Any reduction in the cost of consumer inconvenience could result in greater use of seat belts. While costs and benefits must be considered, research being conducted to produce "near-passive" belt systems could be supported more extensively by DOT.

Concerns over Available Data. It has been noted that DOT's economic analyses rely heavily on laboratory data as opposed to field test data. Decisions based principally on laboratory data often lead to disappointment. Engineers are generally optimistic about the devices they have developed. In many cases, however, they lose sight of the fact that these devices face their ultimate test in the hands of real people, not test dummies, animals, or cadavers. Furthermore, engineers are likely to ignore the fact that these systems generally will be installed, maintained, and operated by nonengineers. The adverse reaction of the public to the ignition interlock system illustrates what can happen when the full range of human behavior is not considered. In fact, it may not be possible to simulate accurately real-world driving habits on test tracks.

Lab and field testing of the passive restraint systems illustrate these concerns. For example, tests show the following results:

- Air bags deploy in crashes in which deployment is designed to occur and do not deploy in lower level crashes.

- The threat of accident in case of inadvertent deployment is not severe.

- Bag deployment poses little threat of injury to adults.

Unfortunately, field tests have yet to provide adequate answers to the following questions:

- In real-world accidents, how effective are air bags in preventing death and injury, especially in small-car crashes? (The latter is an extremely important consideration because it is expected that small cars will soon be making up a larger portion of the U.S. auto population.)

- To what extent would occupants of cars equipped with air bags use lap belts? (It is quite possible that passengers in cars equipped with air bags will be less inclined to use the belts because of a perceived security provided by the bags. This is an important consideration because the data imply that air bags by themselves are effective only in frontal collisions.)

- To what extent will passive belt systems, if utilized, be effective in the field?
- What fraction of the population would defeat the passive belt system by disconnecting or cutting the belts?

Additional Field Testing. Three of the alternatives proposed by the secretary could provide access to the field data that are essential for making a proper decision on passenger restraints. For example, the mandatory passive restraint alternative can be looked on as a huge field test. If passive restraints were mandated and were revealed to be highly effective, it is possible that the reduction in auto-related deaths and injuries could offset the costs. If, on the other hand, the passive systems failed to achieve the expected benefits, the cost of the decision in terms of resources foregone would be vast. Before adopting an industrywide standard, DOT should carefully study its experimental data. Additional field testing could yield significant returns.

The alternative requiring auto manufacturers to offer a passive restraint option for certain cars can be analyzed along similar lines. In this case, the costs might be slightly less, but they would still be sizable, depending on the number of models affected by the proposed rule. The greater the number of models affected, the closer the total resource costs would approach those required if passive restraints were made completely mandatory. The incremental net benefits accruing to this alternative would depend on the frequency of accidents associated with various auto models. Here again, the risk that the passive system might not prove as effective in real-world use as had been expected could make the costs of such a decision extremely great.

In light of the risks attendant with using the first two alternatives as field tests, it is recommended that a smaller-scale, federally sponsored field test of passive restraint systems be conducted. A fleet of 100,000 small cars equipped with air bags should be put on the road as soon as possible. Such a fleet might include a number of automobiles having a *belt* passive restraint system instead of air bags. Experience with this fleet would then provide the data on use and effectiveness that is needed to make a rational decision about passenger restraints. In addition to providing effectiveness data, such a test fleet would also allow manufacturers some experience in install-ing and maintaining the systems before going into full-scale production.

Three alternatives exist for administering such a small-scale test.

Alternative 1. The federal government would receive bids from the auto manufacturers to produce the required number of cars (preferably small models) with passive restraint systems installed. The manufacturer with the lowest bid would put these cars into its dis-tribution system at the *same price* as regularly equipped cars. An advantage of this alternative is that production costs would be mini-mized. Moreover, within limits, the sample could be tailored with respect to geographical area, type of driver, and so forth. On the other hand, dealers might create price differentials between the equipped and the nonequipped cars—for example, refusing to dis-count those having air bags—and, depending on the relative desires of consumers, this could bias the sample.

Alternative 2. As in Alternative 1, the federal government would contract for a given volume of cars equipped with passive restraints but would allow the manufacturer to sell these cars at whatever prices they would bring. This has the advantage not only of producing such cars at their lowest social costs but also of reducing the cost to the federal government (because the contract would take into account the share of the cost the consumer would be willing to bear) and of allocating the equipped cars to those who value them the most. On the other hand, the sample could be biased because persons who would choose to purchase equipped cars may not provide a representative cross-section of all automobile purchasers.

Alternative 3. The federal government could offer a direct cash payment either to a manufacturer upon certification that it had pro-duced and sold a car equipped with a passive restraint or to the con-sumer upon certification that he or she had purchased such a car. By manipulating the amount of the payment, the government could alter the size and composition of the test fleet. This alternative has the advantage of producing the cars at low cost (a manufacturer could specialize in one production run, if it wished), and the equipped cars would be allocated to consumers who valued the restraint system the most. Also, a by-product of a program of partial reimbursement to consumers could be greater awareness on the part of the traveling public of the advantages of restraint systems of various types. On the other hand, there may be biases in the sample, and there would be less certainty with respect to the size and composition of the sam-ple (at least until the start-up phase was over).

These three alternatives contain serious questions that need to be considered carefully before any of them is implemented. Also, as with any field test of this sort, mechanisms would have to be developed to monitor the performance of the systems. Nevertheless, field test alternatives such as these are worthy of further study.

Summary and Conclusions

DOT's economic analysis of the crash protection systems shows that the lap and shoulder restraint system currently installed in most U.S. cars is extremely effective in reducing death and injury when the belts are worn. As the department has noted, the major problem with the current system is that it receives such low use. Accordingly, consideration should be given to passage of mandatory seat belt laws, hard-line advertising campaigns, and improved seat belt design.

If improved utilization of currently available restraint systems cannot be improved on a cost-beneficial basis, the mandatory air bag restraint system may be the best option available. For this reason, any decision by the department should not eliminate further work on this system. The massive costs, however, of placing the system into full-scale production and the risk that the system will not live up to expectations in a real-world environment make the mandating of an air bag system unattractive at this time.

To resolve this dilemma, the department should provide for a test fleet of small cars equipped with air bags in order to obtain more real-world experience with the system. The sooner such a test is undertaken, the sooner an informed decision can be made on this important issue. In considering the final decision, however, DOT should review carefully its benefit-cost analyses and base its decision on the alternative that offers the greatest net social benefits. That is, the social costs of its action should be minimized.

Considerable further activity in this matter has ensued, including an additional filing by the Council on Wage and Price Stability in May 1977, and on June 30, 1977, the secretary of transportation announced a final decision. A performance standard for automatic crash protection will be phased in, applying to large cars in model year 1982, to intermediate and compact size cars in model year 1983, and to subcompacts in model year 1984. The standard does not mandate air bags, but rather permits any passive system; indeed, the passive belt approach appears to be attracting support as a considerably less costly alternative to the air bag.

II. PRODUCT SAFETY

In addition, the secretary decided to seek voluntary industry agreement to produce some cars with automatic crash protection for sale to the public in the 1980 model year. This will be coupled with an intensive monitoring program by the Department of Transportation to oversee implementation plans and to report to the public on the reliability of the available automatic crash protection devices.

PART THREE

Energy, the Environment, and International Trade

8

The Energy Efficiency of Household Appliances

Milton Z. Kafoglis and Robert L. Greene

The Arab oil embargo in 1973 created a major disturbance in the U.S. economy. The price of oil tripled and the nation became aware that its main source of energy was endangered. Many policy prescriptions have been suggested, but disagreement is intense. The debate has centered on the relative merits of policies designed to encourage production versus policies designed to encourage conservation. This study attempts to evaluate a proposal designed to encourage conservation.

The Energy Policy and Conservation Act of 1975 (EPCA)[1] mandates the Federal Energy Administration (FEA) to establish targets for improving the energy efficiency of certain electric and gas appliances. In May 1976, FEA issued proposed regulations for ten classes of consumer appliances, beginning with the 1980 models.[2] These appliances are: refrigerators and refrigerator-freezers, freezers, dishwashers, clothes dryers, water heaters, room air conditioners, home heating equipment (except furnaces), television sets, kitchen ranges and ovens, and clothes washers.

The congressional mandate requires FEA to establish the targets in such a way that the aggregate energy efficiency of all of these products that are manufactured in calendar year 1980 will exceed the aggregate efficiency achieved by such products manufactured in

This chapter is edited from "Energy Conservation Program for Appliances: 10 CFR Part 430," Comments of the Council on Wage and Price Stability before the Federal Energy Administration, June 9, 1976.

[1] P.L. 94–163 (1975).
[2] 41 Fed. Reg. 19977 (May 14, 1976).

calendar year 1972 by at least 20 percent. In addition, FEA must determine aggregate efficiency targets in excess of 20 percent if this is both economically and technologically feasible.

The targets are to be set for individual product lines, and they may vary as long as, in the aggregate, appliances meet the minimum standard of 20 percent, or a higher figure if in FEA's judgment this would be feasible. Of course, some manufacturers may find it more or less costly than average to raise the efficiency of a given product line to the predetermined standard. Moreover, since manufacturers tend to differ in the relative emphasis they give to various product lines, the existence of variable targets by product line may affect some manufacturers more than others.

These targets are "voluntary"; this does not, however, alter the fact that they will have significant economic effects. Under the act, if the administrator of the FEA finds that the target for any individual product line is not likely to be met by 1980, he must promulgate a mandatory standard of energy efficiency for that type or class of product.[3] Any individual appliance sold in interstate commerce would then have to meet that standard. Thus, for example, if a target of a 30 percent efficiency improvement in refrigerators is established now and at a later date it appears that refrigerators are not in fact becoming 30 percent more efficient, this would be the basis for a mandatory standard.[4] Thus, the setting of these "voluntary" targets is extremely important.

FEA should give serious consideration to economic factors in setting both voluntary targets and mandatory standards. In fact, an economic analysis of the energy efficiency targets is contemplated by the Energy Policy and Conservation Act. Under the act, the initial targets must be "economically feasible." Further, any target subsequently prescribed by FEA as a mandatory standard must be "economically justified," a term defined by the act as requiring a cost-benefit analysis of the standard. Since a cost-benefit analysis is required for the prescription of standards, it would be appropriate for FEA to undertake that analysis at the time that the initial energy gets are proposed.[5]

---

[3] EPCA, section 325(a)(4)(B).

[4] FEA may alter targets once set; see EPCA, section 325(a)(3).

[5] Congress's intent that FEA undertake cost-benefit analysis of its proposed conservation measures is also clarified in the Federal Energy Administration Act, P.L. 93–275 (1974), which requires that "the Administrator shall develop analyses of the economic impact of various conservation measures on states or significant sectors thereof."

Overall Concerns about the Proposed Regulation

The FEA proposal raises three major concerns. The first concern is that the agency has not yet completed an economic analysis of these regulations; thus, their inflationary effects are as yet unknown. According to FEA data, in 1975 the total value of shipments of the affected products was more than $10 billion.[6] If the 1975 prices of these appliances were increased by an average of 5 percent—one design cost figure used by FEA—U.S. consumers would incur additional annual costs attributable to the regulation of more than $500 million measured in 1975 dollars.[7] An increase of this magnitude would be significant to the U.S. economy, and thus FEA should prepare a truly comprehensive economic analysis of its prepared action.

The second concern has to do with cost-effectiveness. Although FEA is required by the Energy Policy and Conservation Act to establish a minimum aggregate improvement of 20 percent for these appliances, this aggregate improvement should be accomplished in a cost-effective, or least costly, manner. That is, the public should receive the benefits (increased energy conservation) with the least sacrifice of alternative goods and services. In order to ensure that lowest costs are attained, FEA must weigh the costs of alternative means of achieving the objectives and select the one that achieves these benefits at lowest total costs.

The final concern has to do with benefit-cost analysis. FEA has discretion to establish targets beyond 20 percent if they are both technologically and economically feasible. But targets beyond 20 percent should be established only if an incremental increase in the efficiency figure will increase total benefits by more than total costs to consumers. To reach this objective, FEA should complete a benefit-cost analysis of different improvement targets for each of the appliances and use (marginal) benefit-cost ratios to derive a final aggregate improvement target that is economically efficient.

The principal objective of this study is to provide FEA with suggestions about how these energy-efficiency improvements might be obtained in the most economically efficient manner. The study does not take issue with the mandated 20 percent minimum improvement nor with FEA's authority to promulgate the standard and to set higher

---

[6] Taken from technical reports issued by FEA on each of the affected appliances.

[7] Early data received from FEA indicate that 5 percent is the lowest price increase anticipated for some of the design options expected to be placed on individual appliances to meet the target. Later FEA analysis suggests that 5 percent may overestimate the costs attributable to the regulation.

standards if, in its judgment, such an action would be required by the EPCA.

Concerns with the Proposed Targets

The Federal Energy Administration has issued a series of technical papers relating to each of the ten classes of appliances. These reports contain: (1) proposed ranges for improvement in the energy-efficiency ratio, (2) the range of improved energy efficiency that might be obtained from each of several design options, and (3) the expected increase in price associated with each design option as a percentage of the 1975 base price. In addition, FEA has given a preliminary estimate of $258.1 million as the 1980 increased cost of implementing the standard.[8]

A wide and unresolved discrepancy exists, however, between the costs and benefits projected by FEA and those projected by the manufacturers. For example, the Association of Home Appliance Manufacturers (AHAM) has published data indicating that one year's cost (1981) of meeting these targets would be about $7 billion.[9] This estimate, however, grossly exaggerates the costs. AHAM's costs are based on the presumption that every manufacturer will install every design option on its appliances. In this event, improved efficiency would in some cases far exceed the proposed targets. For example, in the case of refrigerators, AHAM projects the *increase* in price to be $387.50. This increase would be about 155 percent higher than the 1975 base price of $250 for a refrigerator. The improvement in efficiency that would result would be about 143 percent.[10] Such an improvement would be far above the FEA proposed target range for refrigerators of 43 percent to 50 percent.

FEA and the home appliance manufacturing industry should reconcile these differences and derive some realistic targets and cost estimates. Until these differences are reconciled, it would be better for FEA to establish the minimum 20 percent improvement required

---

[8] Correspondence from Alvin A. Cook, Jr., deputy assistant administrator for Economic Impact Analysis of the Federal Energy Administration, to James C. Miller III, assistant director for Government Operations and Research of the Council on Wage and Price Stability, May 25, 1976.

[9] Association of Home Appliance Manufacturers (AHAM), *Federal Energy Estimates of Consumer Cost Impact of Meeting Energy Target Goals* (Washington, D.C., April 7, 1976), p. 1.

[10] The AHAM estimate is based on the erroneous assumption that all the efficiency improvements of each design option are additive and are calculated from the same base. This problem is addressed later in this study and is used here only as an example of issues FEA needs to resolve.

under the act and prescribe further improvements only after a more thorough technical and economic assessment of their impacts has been completed.

As the requirements of the act are structured, two types of economic analyses are relevant for determining the optimal goals for improving energy efficiency. The first is cost-effectiveness analysis, which would provide a framework within which a strategy for reaching a given regulatory objective in the least costly manner could be determined. In the case of the proposed targets, this type of analysis should be applied to the minimum 20 percent improvement required under the act.

To satisfy criteria of economic efficiency, the costs of all alternatives must be considered and balanced. This balance is obtained when the additional costs per British thermal unit (Btu) saved are equal for all the affected appliances. If these marginal costs per Btu saved are not equal, the total cost of meeting the overall target can be lowered by raising the individual targets for those appliances with a low cost per Btu saved and lowering the individual targets for those appliances with a higher cost per Btu saved. This process would be continued until the costs per Btu saved were equal for all appliances, and the 20 percent aggregate improvement was attained. In this manner the cost of reaching the given objective would be minimized.[11]

Further, FEA must determine the economic efficiency of targets beyond 20 percent. That is, should the aggregate improvement target be established at 25 percent, 30 percent, 35 percent, or some other level beyond 20 percent? In this case the proper analysis involves comparing the marginal costs and the marginal benefits of raising the overall standard while meeting at each stage the cost-effectiveness criterion mentioned above.

Since the Energy Policy and Conservation Act requires that the energy improvement from 1972 to 1980 be no less than 20 percent, it is suggested that FEA first employ a cost-effectiveness analysis to establish individual targets that will yield the aggregate 20 percent minimum at the lowest possible cost. This should then be followed by a cost-benefit analysis to determine the extent to which it is economically efficient for the aggregate energy improvement target to be raised beyond 20 percent.

---

[11] The disadvantage of cost-effectiveness analysis is that it does not provide a framework for evaluating the economic efficiency of the goal itself. In this case, however, the 20 percent minimum improvement is required by the Congress and is not at issue here.

To find that combination of individual product targets that will yield at least a 20 percent aggregate reduction in Btu, one must calculate, for each product, the incremental cost per Btu saved at successive levels of energy efficiency. Those improvements that yield the lowest cost per Btu saved at successive levels of energy efficiency should be made first, followed by improvements at those levels that yield the next lowest cost per Btu, and so forth. In this way incremental costs per Btu saved across product lines are kept as nearly equal as possible, and a given aggregate goal is attained at the lowest possible cost. The aggregate level of efficiency can be calculated by weighting the level achieved for each product by the unit sales volume of that product.

This iterative procedure is illustrated in Table 8–1, which employs hypothetical figures. The first improvement would be made to product X_3, for which the incremental cost for an efficiency improvement to the 5 percent level is 0.02 cents; this would be followed by an improvement to product X_5, for which the incremental cost is 0.03 cents. Successive improvements are made in this manner until a weighted aggregate efficiency level of 20 percent has been attained. At this point, the incremental cost per Btu saved will be equal for all products. In the example illustrated in Table 8–1, products X_1 and X_2 would be improved to the 20 percent level, product X_3 to the 25 percent level product X_4 to the 10 percent level, and product X_5 to the 30 percent

TABLE 8–1

HYPOTHETICAL COST PER BTU SAVED AT VARIOUS LEVELS
OF EFFICIENCY, BY PRODUCT

Level of Total Improvement (percent)	Incremental Improvement (percent)	Product (cents)[a]				
		X_1	X_2	X_3	X_4	X_5
5	5	0.15	0.04	0.02	0.15	0.03
10	5	0.20	0.10	0.04	(0.30)	0.05
15	5	0.25	0.20	0.09	0.40	0.15
20	5	(0.30)	(0.30)	0.20	0.50	0.20
25	5	0.35	0.40	(0.30)	0.60	0.25
30	5	0.40	0.50	0.40	0.70	(0.30)

[a] The numbers in parentheses indicate the level at which a weighted aggregate efficiency level of 20 percent is attained at an equal incremental cost per Btu saved for all products.

level. The process of adjustment will stop when the sales-weighted aggregate reaches the minimum 20 percent required by the act.

The cost employed in making these calculations are the estimated increased initial costs for each type of product divided by the estimated lifetime energy savings in Btu for that product. This calculation must be made for each level of improvement and for each product. Illustrative calculations for the first three cells of product X_1 are shown in Table 8–2.

After the minimum aggregate 20 percent improvement for all products combined has been obtained, the analysis should then proceed with a calculation of the benefit-cost ratio for each appliance. The benefit-cost ratios between appliances should be as nearly equal as it is possible to attain if cost-effectiveness criteria have been satisfied and if the price per Btu is assumed to be constant. Finally, the magnitude of these ratios can be used to determine the extent to which improvement beyond 20 percent might be made.

To calculate the benefit-cost ratios, the incremental benefits must first be estimated. To do this, FEA should consider the net reduced operating costs that correspond to the discounted value of the energy saved along with other increased or decreased costs for maintenance of the product attributable to the targets. These incremental benefits for each appliance should be calculated for alternative incremental improvements beyond the target necessary to reach the 20 percent aggregate improvement.

Next, the incremental costs must be estimated. These costs should also be calculated for incremental improvements for each appliance beyond the target necessary to reach the aggregate 20 percent minimum.

Finally, the estimated incremental benefits and costs should be

TABLE 8–2

Illustrative Calculations of the Incremental Costs of Product X_1

Level of Improvement (percent)	Lifetime Btu Savings (thousands)	Total Cost of Improvement (cents)	Incremental Cost (cents)	Incremental Btu (thousands)	Incremental Cost per Btu Saved (cents)
5	10	15	15	10	0.15
10	20	35	20	10	0.20
15	30	60	25	10	0.25

combined to derive a benefit-cost ratio for each of the incremental additions to the minimum target level. As long as these ratios are greater than unity, further improvements in the individual target levels can be considered economically efficient. If the ratio for stricter targets is less than unity, then further improvements in target levels must be judged economically inefficient and inflationary.

Once these ratios are determined, it becomes possible to construct a matrix that shows the benefit-cost ratios for incremental improvements beyond 20 percent for each appliance. By examining the matrix, the optimal target for each appliance can be determined. As noted earlier, as far as possible, the incremental benefit-cost ratios across appliances should be equated and made equal to unity. Thus, as is shown in Table 8–3, the individual product improvements should be 25 percent (20 + 5) for product X_1, 40 percent (20 + 20) for product X_2, 40 percent (25 + 15) for product X_3, 35 percent (10 + 25)

TABLE 8–3

HYPOTHETICAL BENEFIT-COST RATIOS FOR INDIVIDUAL INCREMENTAL
EFFICIENCY IMPROVEMENTS BEYOND MINIMUM REQUIREMENT

Total Incremental Improvements in Individual Targets beyond Minimum Requirement (percent)	Incremental Improvements in Individual Targets beyond Minimum Requirement (percent)	Product[a]				
		X_1	X_2	X_3	X_4	X_5
0	0	6.00	6.00	6.00	6.00	6.00
5	5	1.00	5.00	3.00	5.00	2.00
10	5	0.25	2.00	2.00	4.00	1.00
15	5	0.20	1.50	1.00	3.00	0.50
20	5	0.13	1.00	0.50	2.00	0.25
25	5	0.10	0.75	0.20	1.00	0.12
30	5	0.05	0.50	0.10	0.50	0.08

NOTE: Each benefit-cost ratio represents the most cost-effective alternative set of design options to obtain the incremental 5 percent improvements. From Table 8-1 it is known that the minimal requirements for each product are the following: X_1 is 20 percent, X_2 is 20 percent, X_3 is 25 percent, X_4 is 10 percent, and X_5 is 30 percent.

[a] The benefit-cost ratio of 6 is computed at the minimum requirement for each product. That is, product X_1 with 20 percent improvement, product X_2 with 20 percent improvement, product X_3 with 25 percent improvement, product X_4 with 10 percent improvement, and product X_5 with 30 percent improvement (see Table 8-1 and the note above); the weighted aggregate efficiency improvement reflected across this first line is 20 percent.

for product X_4, and 40 percent (30 + 10) for product X_5. At these levels, the marginal benefit-cost ratios are equal to 1.0.[12]

The aggregate improvement level can be determined from these individual product improvement targets. Such a determination would involve taking a weighted average of the individual improvement target levels. The most appropriate weighting procedure would be to multiply each individual product target level by the projected unit sales of the product. This weighted average would then represent the aggregate improvement level for the appliances as a group.

Concerns Regarding Data

In the process of calculating the benefits and costs needed to complete the above matrices, FEA will have to address certain problems connected with collecting and processing data. The first problem relates to the calculation of energy savings and increased costs. As the targets are now proposed, 1972 is the base from which the 20 percent energy improvement by 1980 is to be measured. For a meaningful economic assessment, however, the relevant benefits and costs are those incurred as the result of incremental changes between 1976 and 1980 model appliances.

In the case of benefits, the effective reduction in energy consumed that is relevant to the analysis is the difference between the energy consumption of the 1976 models and the energy consumption of the 1980 models. For example, assume that in 1972 the energy consumption of an average freezer was about 340,000 Btu a month. Further, assume that by 1980 energy consumption must be reduced 26 percent. This 26 percent reduction would be about 88,400 Btu a month. Suppose, however, that by 1976 manufacturers have already lowered energy consumption 40,000 Btu a month. In this case, the effect of the regulation is to generate benefits of 48,400 Btu a month, not the 88,400 Btu measured from the 1972 base. The same procedures apply to costs. The costs used in the cost-effectiveness and benefit-cost analyses should measure the costs of the regulation by estimating the increase in 1976 appliance prices as a result of the regulations.[13]

---

[12] Ideally, the energy consumption saved should be adjusted for the increased energy used to produce the additional materials needed for the improvement.

[13] This procedure is based on an implicit assumption that no further improvements in energy efficiency would occur between 1976 and 1980 in the absence of the targets. To the extent this assumption is not valid, both benefits and costs of the proposed regulation would be overstated. Optimally, the benefits and costs should be measured as the differences between 1980 models in the absence of the targets and 1980 models with the targets.

Thus, the data that FEA needs to obtain are the energy use of 1972 appliances, the energy use of 1976 models, the projected energy use of the 1980 models, and the projected price increases as a result of the efficiency target levels. Close cooperation between FEA and the industry will be necessary to generate these estimates.

A second consideration is the extent to which price increases may cause the consumer to shift to less energy-efficient alternatives to minimize or avoid increases in initial cost.[14] The mix among models in the same product line that differ in their energy efficiency will have a significant effect on whether a target is met. If increased prices lead consumers to shift to lower-priced, less energy-efficient models in the same product line, an improvement target based on the weighted average of unit sales and predicated on a given product mix would be inaccurate. Consequently, a target of 40 percent improvement may not in fact be met if the proportion of lower-cost, less energy-efficient models increases as a result of consumers' response to the increased price.

The extent to which such shifts occur will depend upon the importance consumers attach to energy costs as a variable in their purchase decisions. The consumer will probably consider several significant variables in making his choice: initial cost (price), operating costs (including energy costs), expected life, appearance, brand loyalty, a manufacturer's reputation, and the nature and length of the warranty. The relative importance of these variables will determine the product mix of brands and models. The effects of both increased price and energy savings must be projected within the framework of all these variables to determine the final product mix that will in fact result. In order to generate this type of data, it will be necessary to complete a demand analysis for each product line through a joint effort by FEA and the industry.

Another factor that might have some bearing on product mix is the industry's competitive structure and the propensity of individual firms to meet the targets. FEA itself recognizes that these targets will have different impacts on different producers.[15] Thus, some manufacturers will be able to meet the targets with lower increases in prices than other manufacturers. Consequently, one would expect a change in the relative prices of various appliances and a subsequent change in product mix. This change, as it affects the weighting system, will also

---

[14] For example, some dishwasher owners could decide to wash dishes by hand rather than replace a dishwasher at the higher price. The net effect could be greater energy consumption.

[15] 41 Fed. Reg. 19977.

affect the ability of the industry to conform to a specific standard. To adjust for this problem, members of the industry should each cooperate with FEA by supplying cost and price data needed to analyze adequately this aspect of the problem.[16]

As the targets and their system of implementation are proposed, a "free rider" problem may develop. The targets proposed by FEA are voluntary and "the degree of acceptance of these targets and the specific proposed measures to implement them are at the initiative of affected manufacturers and not the FEA."[17] The principal means of making the targets effective will be through labeling rules to be established separately by the Federal Trade Commission. These rules will require manufacturers to have their products tested and to label the energy costs of their appliances. Thus, consumers will be able to compare "first cost" and operating expenses, and labeling requirements will create some degree of self-enforcement through the purchasing decisions of consumers.

This discipline may not, however, be sufficient to force manufacturers, in the aggregate, to meet the targets. Moreover, marketing experts report that consumers tend to overemphasize first costs and to underemphasize or overlook completely operating expenses. To the extent that consumers behave in this manner, a manufacturer will find it in its interest to avoid making the improvements in order to keep the initial price low. If one manufacturer chooses to make the improvements in order to help meet the industry target and others do not, then this manufacturer may lose its market share and realize lower profits. In short, a "let George do it" attitude may prevail, and the industry may fall short of its target.[18]

To the extent that some manufacturers make an effort to meet the targets while others do not, a serious question of equity arises. If complete voluntary cooperation cannot be achieved, FEA may be

---

[16] Some of the data that should be collected (for example, projected 1980 prices) might currently be deemed confidential business data. FEA should consider the possible anticompetitive effects (principally on future price-setting for 1980) when making any decision about whether to make this data part of a public record in the current proceeding.

[17] 41 Fed. Reg. 19979.

[18] As an FEA consultant's report states: "Because of the potential economic distortions that could occur within both the domestic industrial structure and with the import competing framework, it appears that anything less than 100 percent voluntary cooperation with appropriate import regulations will have inherent economic biases that would quickly lead to the voluntary compliers being forced to renege on their commitment." See InfoDyne Systems Corporation, *Economic Impact Study of the Appliance Efficiency Program* (Washington, D.C., June 30, 1975), p. 135.

forced either to adopt mandatory standards or to impose some form of fine or penalty on firms that do not comply, making their costs the same as or possibly higher than those of firms that do comply. Once compliance is achieved, the fine would disappear.

Whether voluntary or mandated, however, the targets may impose an "economic welfare" loss on those consumers who would in fact prefer appliances having lower first costs. It is likely that such welfare losses would fall most heavily on lower income classes. These impacts should be balanced against the long-term gains to the community that would result from energy conservation.

Summary and Conclusions

This study has attempted to offer suggestions about how FEA might implement energy-efficient improvements in an economically efficient manner and still fulfill the congressional mandate set forth in the Energy Policy and Conservation Act. The procedure proposed here uses economic analysis in determining appropriate targets and aggregate improvement levels.

Household appliances represent an important sector of the U.S. economy. Any regulations that would have a significant impact on this sector, such as those proposed by FEA, should be carefully analyzed to determine their inflationary impact. Consequently, FEA should complete a comprehensive economic analysis before promulgating the final improvement targets for each product line and the final aggregate improvement target. Finally, it is hoped that the major disagreements between FEA and the appliance industry will be reconciled, that the "free-rider" problem will be reduced or eliminated, and that a set of economically efficient improvement targets will be established.

On April 11, 1978, the Department of Energy (DOE) published energy-efficiency targets for thirteen products.[19] *The targets were developed separately for each product and are designed to achieve the maximum percentage improvement that is "economically and technologically feasible." The aggregate improvement in energy efficiency if these targets are met by 1980 is about 28 percent above the 1972 level.*

The cost-effectiveness and benefit-cost analyses suggested in the Council on Wage and Price Stability (CWPS) study were not per-

---

[19] 43 Fed. Reg. 15147.

formed. The procedures that were employed ensure only that total *benefits exceed* total *costs for each product, but they do not ensure an optimal level of improvement (Table 8–3) or a cost-effective mix of product targets (Table 8–1). The maximum improvement that is "economically and technologically feasible" could result in targets that impose incremental costs in excess of incremental benefits. Moreover, the procedure does not ensure cost-effectiveness—that is, that the incremental cost per Btu saved is the same for all products. Notwithstanding these shortcomings, the DOE analysis represented a serious effort to establish targets that rely on more than mere technological feasibility.*

9

Emission Standards for New Motorcycles

Roger J. Mallet

In early 1974 the Environmental Protection Agency (EPA) first announced its intention to establish emission regulations for new motorcycles based on the goals of the Clean Air Act of 1970. The agency was particularly concerned with the impact of motorcycle emissions in five regions of the country where attainment of the national air quality standards appeared most difficult. By 1975 EPA had proposed motorcycle emission standards for model years 1979 and beyond for three major pollutants—carbon monoxide, hydrocarbons, and nitrogen oxides. Although less stringent interim standards were put forth, the final standards proposed were at the same levels as the existing statutory emission standards for light-duty vehicles. Even though the estimated cost of reducing emissions on a unit basis was much higher for motorcycles than for automobiles, a major premise underlying EPA's proposed action was that all vehicles should conform to the same level of allowable emissions. EPA acknowledged, however, that the standards eventually adopted would greatly depend on the technical feasibility and cost-effectiveness of known emission control systems, as well as congressional consideration of future emission levels for new automobiles.

In October 1975 EPA proposed regulations for all new motorcycles designed for street or highway use that would eventually set permanent standards for crankcase and exhaust emissions of carbon monoxide, nitrogen oxides, and hydrocarbons equivalent to those already

This chapter is edited from "Emission Regulations for New Motorcycles," Comments of the Council on Wage and Price Stability before the Environmental Protection Agency, Office of Mobile Source Air Pollution Control (AW-455), December 10, 1975.

established for automobiles and small trucks.[1] The standards would be implemented in two steps—with a January 1, 1978, deadline for compliance with phase-in standards and a January 1, 1980, deadline for compliance with more rigorous permanent standards.[2]

EPA's stated rationale for establishing the proposed emission standards is that "all vehicles used for public transportation should, to the extent feasible, be controlled to the same levels of allowable emissions of air pollutants." Yet, EPA acknowledges that it has not made any finding that the proposed standards, as applied to motorcycles, are "cost effective, technologically feasible or fully in the public interest."[3] Thus, EPA intends to apply to new motorcycles the same emission standards developed for automobiles and small trucks unless data are developed to indicate that such standards are "not feasible due to technological or cost restraints."[4]

This study analyzes the proposal's inflationary impact and concludes that the probable costs of the proposal would exceed its probable benefits. It also raises questions about whether the proposed stringent standards for 1980 might not undermine the efforts of EPA toward its ultimate goal—namely, cleaner air. The analysis arrives at three principal findings. First, even with the assumed increases in the sales and use of motorcycles, motorcycle emissions will not become a significant source of air pollution on a national level, although they may be important in a few localities. Thus, the proposal will have a limited impact on improving the level of air quality. Second, as EPA's own estimates indicate, the proposed standards will not be as cost-effective for motorcycles (and certainly not for all types and sizes of on-road motorcycles) as the equivalent standards for automobiles have been. In other words, there are less costly means of reducing pollution from such vehicles. Third, the price increases that

---

[1] 40 Fed. Reg. 49496 (October 22, 1975).

[2] The interim 1978–1979 standards proposed by EPA were 17 grams per kilometer for carbon monoxide (CO), 1.2 grams per kilometer for nitrogen oxides (NO_x), and a sliding displacement dependency standard for hydrocarbons (HC) of 5.0 grams per kilometer for those motorcycles with engine displacement of less than 170 cubic centimeters, 5 to 14 grams per kilometer for engine displacements between 170 and 750 cubic centimeters, and 14 grams per kilometer above 750 cubic centimeters. For model year 1980 and later, the EPA proposed the substantially more stringent standards of 2.1 grams per kilometer for CO, 0.25 grams per kilometer for NO_x, and 0.25 grams per kilometer for HC.

[3] 40 Fed. Reg. 49496.

[4] Because of the lack of adequate cost information on the control of motorcycle emissions, EPA's cost estimates are to a great degree "best guess" estimates. One purpose of the current comment period of this rule making is to develop more precise information.

will result from the proposal will likely cause a greater transfer of new motorcycle demand to off-road motorcycles (which are exempt from the Clean Air Act and the proposed regulations) than EPA has estimated.

For these reasons, EPA is urged not to implement the proposed emission standards. EPA should first consider whether motorcycle emissions are a sufficient national problem to require regulation. If the answer to that inquiry is in the affirmative, EPA should then consider promulgating standards applicable only to the types of motorcycles and motorcycle use for which they are cost-effective.

Impact of Proposed Regulations on Air Quality

The proposed emission standards, even if totally effective, would achieve only a slight improvement in air quality at the national level. Further, the proposal's impact on the air quality of certain urban areas is likely to be less than predicted by EPA.

EPA calculates that between 1975 and 1990 total motorcycle emissions, if uncontrolled, would increase more than 100 percent. EPA's analysis of the potential benefits of the proposal, however, indicates that, of total nationwide emissions in 1980, uncontrolled motorcycle emissions would still represent only a small percentage of total hydrocarbons and carbon monoxide emitted by pollution sources. As of 1974, there were 4.9 million registered motorcycles in the United States. EPA estimates that there will be approximately 7.6 million such vehicles registered in 1980 and 12.3 million by 1990. Of total nationwide emissions, EPA estimates that in 1970 motorcycles contributed only 0.15 percent of total hydrocarbons and 0.17 percent of total carbon monoxide.[5] By 1980, these figures are expected to grow to 0.7 percent and 1.3 percent, respectively, based on anticipated increases in vehicle ownership.[6] This low level of pollution contribution would result even though the sales, use, and emissions of motor-

---

[5] These estimates are based on the number and types of registered motorcycles. Excluded are off-road motorcycles that are not registered for highway and street use, and that EPA cannot regulate under the Clean Air Act, but that contribute significantly to air pollution, particularly in California where approximately 27 percent of the bikes sold in the state during 1974 were of this class. The proposed emission regulations would not apply to new motorcycles with an engine displacement of less than 50 cubic centimeters.

[6] It appears that the percentage figures will grow over time primarily because other sources will be controlled to a much greater degree than motorcycles. The use of percentage increases of this nature overstates the actual impact of motorcycle emissions. That is, the lower the level of total emissions, the higher will be the percentages attributable to motorcycle emissions.

cycles are likely to increase, and even though individual motor-cycles have higher emission levels than individual cars.[7]

In proposing the regulations, EPA is basing its position largely on the effect of the proposal on the air quality in certain urban areas. On the basis of projections of overall air quality and the density of motorcycle ownership EPA identifies nine regions where motorcycle emissions could contribute to air quality problems by 1985. Six regions are in California—Los Angeles, San Francisco–Oakland, San Diego, Sacramento, the San Joaquin Valley, and the southeast desert region. The other three regions are also in the West—Phoenix-Tucson, Salt Lake City, and Denver. Nevertheless, a detailed analysis of one such area, Los Angeles, raises considerable question about the need for the standard even in these regions.

In the case of Los Angeles, the EPA estimates that in the late 1970s motorcycles will contribute 5 percent of total permissible hydrocarbon pollution. This figure is based on the number of regis-tered motorcycles in the area as well as the estimated average number of miles the respective vehicle types are driven annually. Further, the estimate is based on the presumption that the use of motorcycles in the Los Angeles area is similar, for purposes of measuring pollu-tion estimates, to the use of other light-duty vehicles.[8] This assump-tion, however, is questionable.

A 1975 survey by the Gallup organization revealed that actual urban usage of motorcycles may be considerably less than that im-plied by the number of vehicles registered by persons living within city limits.[9] The survey revealed that nationally 35 percent of total mileage driven by all motorcycles was off-road (39 percent for those vehicles owned by Los Angeles residents). This would imply that a substantial portion of the pollution attributable to motorcycles occurs off streets and off highways, and presumably, therefore, *out-side* the city or at least outside the inner core of the urban area.

---

[7] New 1976 motorcycles emitted, on the average, twice as much carbon monoxide and six times as many hydrocarbons per mile as new 1976 automobiles. These figures will increase to factors of ten and twenty, respectively, when new statutory standards scheduled for 1978 model automobiles and small trucks are implemented.

[8] EPA states that because "motorcycles are used in the urban area in a manner similar to light-duty-vehicles (*i.e.*, for the purpose of transportation of persons on streets or highways) standards for motorcycle emissions are being proposed at the same level as those established for light-duty-vehicles." Environmental Protection Agency, "Draft Environmental Impact Statement," prepared for the emission regulations for new motorcycles, 1975.

[9] Gallup Organization, *Survey of Motorcycle Ownership, Usage and Maintenance* (Newport Beach, Calif.: Motorcycle Industry Council, January 1975).

Furthermore, only 34 percent of those surveyed in Los Angeles used their motorcycles to commute to work (another 10 percent to commute to school). The average one-way commuting distance in such instances was six miles. Of the motorcycle riders that commuted, only 44 percent of those surveyed entered downtown business or industrial areas, whereas a high of 72 percent commuted through suburban or residential areas. Therefore, for the 34 percent of the Los Angeles residents who owned motorcycles and used their vehicles to commute to work, less than half entered the more congested areas of the city.[10]

Consequently, how much urban pollution is caused by motorcycles—even by motorcycles registered in Los Angeles—is unclear.[11] Since EPA is weighing the urban pollution question heavily, and to a large measure is basing the proposed emission standard on the pollution problems of a few urban areas, the agency should make a better effort to determine the answers to this question.

Cost-Effectiveness of Proposed Regulations

EPA has prepared an economic analysis of the proposal that presents some estimates of the costs associated with the proposed emission standards. This study offers a further analysis of the proposal's impact. As described below, the proposal will produce significantly different cost-effectiveness results for different classes of motorcycles. Moreover, the proposal's cost burden will fall most heavily on the purchasers of those motorcycles that create the least amount of pollution.

A principal reason for the variation in cost-effectiveness among motorcycle types is that the emission characteristics and pollution

---

[10] According to Gallup, the 34 percent figure for motorcycle commuters refers to those who use their bikes on a "regular basis" during good weather. It should be noted that these percentages do not clearly indicate the actual usage level because the weather is a critical factor in selecting this mode of transportation. For commuting to work, the survey found that, for the twenty working days prior to the interview, the median number of round trips to work was only ten. The respective number for school commuters was eight round trips. Thus, the 34 percent figure is in all likelihood overstated. There is no statement about the prevailing weather conditions at the time of the survey, although the survey was conducted during the months of May and June.

[11] A person residing in Los Angeles, for example, may use his vehicle only for weekend pleasure driving to the seashore or mountains. Consequently, although the vehicle is registered in the city, the bulk of the mileage driven may be outside the city. EPA estimates would appear to have more credibility for national or regional levels of pollution but would appear to weaken considerably when city estimates are determined by place of vehicle registration.

control equipment costs for motorcycles vary according to engine type and displacement. For purposes of this discussion, motorcycle types can be classed as "four-stroke" or "two-stroke," and as "large" (greater than 170 cubic centimeters of displacement) or "small" (less than 170 cubic centimeters). Since emission characteristics and estimated pollution control costs vary among these motorcycle types, three observations can be made. First, the amount of emission varies by cycle: the two-stroke motorcycle averages eight to ten times more hydrocarbon pollution per mile than a four-stroke motorcycle of comparable size; on the other hand, a large motorcycle emits greater carbon monoxide pollution than a smaller one of the same type. Second, the annual use of large motorcycles is generally greater than that of small motorcycles; thus, the capital cost of emission control systems can be depreciated over more mileage for the large cycles. Third, the required level of sophistication, and thus the cost, for pollution control equipment varies with the type of motorcycle.

The EPA estimates that the proposed standards will cost purchasers of motorcycles between $304 million and $665 million during the five-year period of regulation—that is, from 1978 to 1982. EPA estimates that the 1978 standards will cost between $20 and $40 a motorcycle—with all two-stroke motorcycles and large four-stroke cycles requiring modifications to meet the hydrocarbon standard. The 1980 standard is estimated by EPA to cost between $50 and $130 per cycle—with the lower side of the cost range in all likelihood applying to small motorcycles and the larger figure applying to large motorcycles. EPA's detailed cost-effectiveness comparison for the various types of motorcycles is presented in its economic assessment of the proposed regulation. These same data are presented here in Tables 9–1 and 9–2, with the single difference being that the figures are presented in tons of pollutant controlled over the life of the cycle and in cost per ton of pollutant controlled.

Table 9–1 shows the varying impact of the proposed hydrocarbon standard on the four classes of motorcycles. The table indicates that in terms of cost the proposed 1980 standard would be most effective for the large two-stroke motorcycles, for which the costs per ton of hydrocarbon controlled would range from $77 to $386. On the other hand, the class of motorcycles least effectively regulated by the 1980 standard would be the small four-stroke motorcycles. In this case, it would cost between $1,777 and $9,060 to regulate a ton of hydrocarbons.

The data in Tables 9–1 and 9–2 can also be used to show that the EPA proposal is significantly less cost-effective for motorcycles than for light-duty vehicles (that is, automobiles and light-duty trucks). EPA currently estimates that the average cost of control per ton of hydrocarbons for light-duty vehicles under the interim 1977 standards to be $303, with the cost increasing to $437 when the new federal statutory standards are implemented.[12] These figures are substantially less than those estimated for every class of motorcycle for 1980, except perhaps the large two-stroke cycle.[13] Similar cost figures are presented in Table 9–2 for control of motorcycle emissions of carbon monoxide. Compared with the average cost of control for light-duty vehicles of $41 a ton, the control of motorcycle emission of carbon monoxide is relatively more expensive than the control of hydrocarbons. Because of this significant difference, EPA should reconsider whether the proposed standards can be justified on the ground that they should be similar to the standards adopted for light-duty vehicles.

Moreover, from the data in Table 9–1, it can be shown that—at least for the four-stroke motorcycles—EPA's proposed standards for 1980 would be a less cost-effective means of controlling hydrocarbon emissions than several alternative technologies that have been employed for controlling automobile and gasoline station hydrocarbon emissions.

In conclusion, the proposed 1980 standards for motorcycles are significantly less cost-effective, at least for the small two-stroke motorcycles and the four-stroke motorcycles, than those associated with light-duty vehicles and, perhaps, with other techniques for controlling emissions from other sources. This is an especially noteworthy finding because the proposal's cost burden falls most heavily on motorcycles that create the least amount of pollution.

According to EPA's analysis, 59 percent of the registered vehicles are four-stroke vehicles, whereas the remaining 41 percent are two-stroke bikes. As Table 9–3 indicates for California, however, the two-stroke bikes account for approximately 83 percent of the total hydrocarbon pollution from motorcycles operated on streets and highways. Given the estimated level and cost of controls, as well as

---

[12] Environmental Protection Agency, *Economic Assessment of the Proposed 1978 Light Duty Truck's Emissions Standards* (1974). The cost figures in this analysis are broken down by pollutants. Such a breakdown was apparently not possible in EPA's analysis for motorcycles. To the extent that this difference exists, any motorcycle cost comparisons presented would be overstated.

[13] This depends on whether one accepts the lower or the higher cost estimates for motorcycles. On the other hand, EPA estimates that the marginal cost per ton of hydrocarbon controlled for light-duty vehicles, going from the interim standard to the pending 1978 standard, would be approximately $515.

TABLE 9-1
Cost-Effectiveness of Hydrocarbon Control for Motorcycles

Standard	Small Two-Stroke[a]		Large Two-Stroke[b]		Small Four-Stroke[a]		Large Four-Stroke[b]	
	Tons controlled over life of cycle[c]	Cost per ton controlled (dollars)	Tons controlled over life of cycle[c]	Cost per ton controlled (dollars)	Tons controlled over life of cycle[c]	Cost per ton controlled (dollars)	Tons controlled over life of cycle[c]	Cost per ton controlled (dollars)
1978 standard (assumed first cost of $30 and 15 percent fuel economy increases)[d]	0.04	634	0.15	47	—[e]	—[e]	—[e]	—[e]
1980 standard (assumed incremental first cost of $20)[f]	0.06	317	0.26	77	0.01	1,777	0.05	389
1980 standard (assumed incremental first cost of $100)[f]	0.06	1,585	0.26	386	0.01	9,060	0.05	1,927

NOTE: Costs given are for modifications that will control both hydrocarbons and carbon monoxide. It is not possible to determine the cost of controlling only one pollutant.

^a For motorcycles less than 170 cubic centimeters, the assumed life is five years.

^b For motorcycles greater than 170 cubic centimeters, the assumed life is eight years.

^c Amounts controlled are based on reductions in pollutant attributable to respective standard and on 12,000 kilometers driven for cycles less than 170 cubic centimeters and 30,000 kilometers for cycles greater than 170 cubic centimeters.

^d Discounted fuel savings are $4.90 for cycles less than 170 cubic centimeters and $23.11 for cycles greater than 170 cubic centimeters.

^e For four-stroke motorcycles, no modifications will be necessary to meet 1978 hydrocarbon standards.

^f First-cost estimates for 1980 standards range from $50 to $130. Incremental hydrocarbon costs are used and account for $30 spent per motorcycle to meet 1978 standards.

SOURCE: Environmental Protection Agency, "Inflation Impact Analysis of the Motorcycle Emissions Standard" (1975), Table F-2.

TABLE 9-2

Cost-Effectiveness of Carbon Monoxide Control for Motorcycles

Standard	Small Two-Stroke[a]		Large Two-Stroke[b]		Small Two-Stroke[a]		Large Two-Stroke[b]	
	Tons controlled over life of cycle[c]	Cost per ton controlled (dollars)	Tons controlled over life of cycle[c]	Cost per ton controlled (dollars)	Tons controlled over life of cycle[c]	Cost per ton controlled (dollars)	Tons controlled over life of cycle[c]	Cost per ton controlled (dollars)
1978 standard (assumed first cost of $30 and 15 percent fuel economy increases)[d]	—[e]	—[e]	0.18	38	—[e]	—[e]	0.18	38
1980 standard (assumed incremental first cost of $20)[f]	0.09	209	0.49	41	0.09	209	0.09	41
1980 standard (assumed incremental first cost of $100)[f]	0.09	1,053	0.49	202	0.09	1,053	0.09	202

NOTE: Costs given are for modifications that will control both hydrocarbons and carbon monoxide. It is not possible to determine the cost of controlling only one pollutant.

[a] For motorcycles less than 170 cubic centimeters, assumed life is five years.

[b] For motorcycles greater than 170 cubic centimeters, assumed life is eight years.

[c] Amounts controlled are based on reductions in pollutant attributable to respective standard and on 12,000 kilometers driven for cycles less than 170 cubic centimeters and 30,000 for cycles greater than 170 cubic centimeters.

[d] Discounted fuel savings are $4.90 for cycles less than 170 cubic centimeters and $23.11 for cycles greater than 170 cubic centimeters.

[e] For motorcycles less than 170 cubic centimeters, no modifications will be necessary to meet 1978 carbon monoxide standards.

[f] First-cost estimates for 1980 standards range from $50 to $130. Incremental hydrocarbon costs are used and account for $30 spent per motorcycle to meet 1978 standards.

SOURCE: Environmental Protection Agency, "Inflation Impact Analysis of the Motorcycle Emissions Standard," Table F-3.

TABLE 9-3

PERCENTAGE BREAKDOWN OF MOTORCYCLE HYDROCARBON POLLUTION FOR LOS ANGELES BY MODEL, ENGINE TYPE, AND DISPLACEMENT

Type of Motorcycle[a]	Engine Type and Displacement	Percentage of Total Motorcycles	Average Annual Mileage	Percentage of Total Mileage	Hydrocarbon Pollution per Kilometer	Percentage of Total Hydrocarbon Pollution
Street (41)	2-Stroke (<170 cc.)	5	2,500	3.78	8.0	5.13
	2-Stroke (>170 cc.)	11	4,100	13.65	12.5	28.92
	4-Stroke (<170 cc.)	3	3,100	2.81	1.1	0.50
	4-Stroke (>170 cc.)	22	4,700	31.30	1.8	9.54
Dual-purpose (36)	2-Stroke (<170 cc.)	11	2,300	7.66	8.0	10.36
	2-Stroke (>170 cc.)	10	3,600	10.90	12.5	23.08
	4-Stroke (<170 cc.)	7	2,400	5.08	1.1	0.95
	4-Stroke (>170 cc.)	8	4,200	10.17	1.8	3.10
Off-road (23)	2-Stroke (<170 cc.)	10	2,200	6.66	8.0	9.03
	2-Stroke (>170 cc.)	6	2,200	4.00	12.5	8.46
	4-Stroke (<170 cc.)	4	2,200	2.66	1.1	0.50
	4-Stroke (>170 cc.)	2	2,200	1.33	1.8	0.41
Total		100[b]		100.00		100.00[b]

[a] Numbers in parentheses are the percentage breakdown of the total number of motorcycles in Los Angeles by type of motorcycle.

[b] Components do not sum to 100 percent because of rounding.

SOURCES: Gallup Organization, Survey of Motorcycle Ownership, Usage and Maintenance (Newport Beach, Calif.: Motorcycle Industry Council, January 1975), p. 16. For the average mileage by model, engine type, and engine displacement, ibid., pp. 30–31. For the hydrocarbon pollution per kilometer by model, engine type, and engine displacement, see Environmental Protection Agency, "Draft Environmental Impact Statement," prepared for the emission regulation for new motorcycles (1975), p. 15.

the composition of registered motorcycles, the owners of four-stroke vehicles would be paying dearly for their relatively small contribution toward cleaner air.

Impact of Price Increases on Motorcycle Demand

EPA estimates that the proposed standards will cause a price increase for motorcycles of between 4.9 percent and 15.2 percent. The largest percentage price increase is expected to be incurred by the small vehicles, which will suffer a greater decline in sales than the larger, more expensive machines. The decline in sales itself will cause some of the price increase. EPA estimates that "approximately two-thirds of the [average] cost increase can be attributed to the emission control systems with the remainder associated with the shift in sales." This implicit assumption by EPA that the price increase for small motorcycles will drive consumers away from the motorcycle market entirely is open to question. It is equally possible that some consumers who cannot afford higher-priced small cycles will move to off-road vehicles.

The socioeconomic characteristics of motorcycle owners suggest that income considerations might well be an important determinant of motorcycle sales. According to a recent Gallup survey for the Motorcycle Industry Council, 50 percent of all owners are less than twenty-four years old and 36 percent are less than twenty. Although the median income of the owner is $15,000, the average or mean income (which is not provided) must be substantially less, because the age distribution is skewed toward the younger age groups. Another interesting statistic provided by the survey is that, although only 23 percent of those polled had off-road bikes, 35 percent of all mileage driven by the three classes of bikes—street, dual-purpose, and off-road—was off roads. Since only 39 percent of those polled nationally used their bikes for commuting to school or work—the same figure for Los Angeles was 34 percent—it can be assumed that one of the major reasons people purchase motorcycles is for recreation. The low income and young age of the majority of owners, as well as the purpose of ownership, would indicate that the consideration of price would be weighed heavily by the average purchaser. This would seem to be the case particularly for the less expensive and much more popular smaller motorcycles.

Sales figures on motorcycles over the 1973–1974 period, when prices increased dramatically, show the possible direction of changes in demand, particularly for the smallest and cheapest bikes (those less

TABLE 9–4

PERCENTAGE CHANGE IN MOTORCYCLE SALES BY VEHICLE SIZE, 1973–1974

Engine Displacement (cubic centimeters)	Percentage Change in Units Sold		Percentage Increase in Retail Prices for Total Motorcycles
	On-road motorcycles	Total motorcycles	
Less than 125	−88.5	−39.4	27
125–349	−41.5	−12.1	19
350–449	−25.4	−23.2	17
450–749	−21.2	−20.6	16
750 and greater	3.5	3.6	30

than 349 cubic centimeters), which accounted for 60 percent of total unit sales in 1974. In 1974, total motorcycle sales declined by 23 percent over the previous year. The decline was not the same for all categories of motorcycles, however. Greater sales reductions occurred for the smaller bikes. Motorcycles with less than 125 cubic centimeters experienced the greatest reduction, whereas the largest motorcycles (those greater than 750 cubic centimeters) actually showed an increase in sales of 3.5 percent (see Table 9–4).

It is particularly interesting to compare the 1973–1974 sales figures of on-road vehicles with those of off-road vehicles for the smallest two classes (those less than 349 cubic centimeters).[14] The off-road bikes, which are substantially cheaper than their on-road counterparts, averaged an increase in price of 35 percent. The street bikes averaged an increase of 39 percent. The number of off-road bikes sold, however, declined substantially less than the number of on-road bikes—a 19 percent decline in sales for off-road bikes compared with a 58 percent decline for on-road bikes.[15] Thus, the available data would appear to suggest that the purchasers of the smaller vehicles are very conscious of price increases, and they are likely to seek a cheaper or inferior substitute. In view of the variety of bikes available and the way bikes are used, a likely substitute may well be an off-road motorcycle, which EPA cannot currently regulate.

---

[14] This group accounted for 92 percent of total off-road vehicles in 1974.

[15] The comparison does not include combination or dual-purpose motorcycles. The sale of dual-purpose vehicles in 1974 declined by approximately 20 percent over the previous year.

TABLE 9–5

Two-Stroke and Off-Road Motorcycles as a Percentage of Total Units Sold, 1969–1974
(percent)

Type and Year	Nationwide	California
Two-stroke		
1969	38	n.a.
1970	40	n.a.
1971	40	n.a.
1972	44	45
1973	47	46
1974	53	50
Off-road		
1972	17	23
1973	19	29
1974	20	27

n.a.: Not available.
SOURCES: For 1969–1971 data, Motorcycle Industry Council, *Manufacturer's Shipment Reporting System Annual Statistical Report* (Newport Beach, Calif., 1973 and 1974); for 1972–1974 data, Southwest Research Institute, *Exhaust Emissions from Uncontrolled Vehicles and Related Equipment Using Internal Combustion Engines* (San Antonio, Tex., March 1973), p. 51.

Another possibility that EPA downplayed in its economic analysis is that purchasers of dual-purpose bikes will switch to off-road, or dirt, bikes. Most of the dual-purpose bikes sold in 1974 (90 percent) were less than 349 cubic centimeters. In fact, dual-purpose bikes less than 349 cubic centimeters accounted for 35 percent of all motorcycles sold in 1974. The possibility that these purchasers may shift to dirt vehicles is a problem that deserves more analysis.

Over the last few years, there has been a clearly discernible trend toward dirt bikes—as well as toward two-stroke vehicles, which are generally associated with dirt bikes (see Table 9–5). It can be argued that the larger percentage price increases for the smaller two-stroke vehicles may hasten the trend toward less expensive off-road vehicles, which have been growing steadily in popularity. This possibility is particularly strong in the case of dual-purpose vehicles. In 1974, the weighted average retail price for off-road motorcycles, for the two size classes less than 349 cubic centimeters, was $653; the comparable price for dual-purpose vehicles of the same two size classes was

$758.[16] If it is assumed that the dual-purpose vehicles will incur the lower estimated cost of $50 in 1980 for pollution controls, the price would rise on the average to $808. Thus, what was originally a 16 percent differential in price will rise to 24 percent. If the upper cost limit of $130 is assumed, the price differential would increase to 36 percent. The question to be asked is whether the majority of purchasers of dual-purpose bikes would be willing to pay this differential for the convenience of riding the vehicle on the road occasionally. As the recent Gallup survey clearly indicates, an estimated 20 percent of the owners of dual-purpose motorcycles never use their vehicles for street riding, and 37 percent of the owners attributed less than a quarter of their driving to street usage.

Consequently, a change at the lower end of the product spectrum to the use of dirt bikes may not only present EPA with a regulatory dilemma but it may also negate to a large degree the total overall benefits expected from the regulation. Such a change in usage may create an even worse problem for areas such as Los Angeles and San Francisco—the largest population centers in California with the worst pollution problems—because 24 percent of the bikes owned are already off-road vehicles. In fact, 27 percent of the cycles sold in California in 1974 were off-road vehicles. Thus, one could argue that, if the trend toward off-road vehicles continues and if it is stimulated by the proposed regulation, by 1980 more than one-third of the new bikes sold in California will fall outside the purview of EPA's control anyway. Since the more polluting two-stroke motorcycle is generally associated with off-road bikes, any gains achieved in controlling on-street cycle pollution may be greatly offset by the growth of off-street vehicles. If this were to occur, the net gain in clean air would be substantially reduced.

Conclusion

EPA should reconsider its proposed emission control standards for motorcycles. The actual amount of total pollutants controlled in urban areas may well be considerably smaller than the amount calculated by EPA. More important, the estimated 1980 costs for controlling emissions from certain motorcycles appear to be very high compared with the cost-effectiveness of regulating other sources of air pollution. Even if EPA determines that action in this area is required for the public health, it should pursue control of only those types of

---

[16] Motorcycle Industry Council, *Manufacturer's Shipment Reporting System Annual Statistical Report* (Newport Beach, Calif., 1974).

motorcycles for which regulation is as efficient as that applied to other sources of air pollution.

If EPA does choose to implement a regulation controlling motorcycle emissions, it should limit the level of the standards to those proposed for 1978 until more definitive cost figures are established for the generally less polluting four-stroke vehicles. In the meantime, it should encourage those few states that will have urban pollution problems with motorcycles to pass their own emission standards for these vehicles. This policy would reduce, at the minimum, the 1978 levels of motorcycle pollution of hydrocarbons and carbon monoxide by 30 and 20 percent, respectively. Such a policy would not be unduly discriminatory toward a particular firm or technology because the net estimated costs are limited. Furthermore, it would limit the potential of stimulating greater sales of off-road motorcycles, which are generally more polluting. This possibility should be a major consideration in the EPA's final determination.

The EPA is directed to achieve certain levels of air quality, and areas such as California may have difficulty attaining these levels. The benefits that would be achieved because of the proposed motorcycle regulation, however, appear to be extremely limited and, as the regulation is currently being proposed, the estimated costs appear to be excessive.

The Environmental Protection Agency eventually adopted emission standards for new motorcycles in January 1977.[17] *The standards adopted by the agency were substantially less stringent than those originally proposed in the notice of proposed rule making on which the Council on Wage and Price Stability commented.*

In adopting the final motorcycle emission regulation, EPA stated that the general responses that it received on the proposed regulation, as well as its own evaluation, indicated that the 1978 standards were technically and economically achievable but that the "statutory standards were not technically feasible as early as 1980, and that control to that level would not be cost effective."[18] *The agency therefore adopted the 1978 standards as proposed (the standard for nitrogen oxides was deleted, however, since it was determined that these emissions were negligible). The standards for 1980 and beyond were substantially loosened, however, compared with those originally proposed.*

---

[17] 42 Fed. Reg. 1122 (January 5, 1977).

[18] The "statutory standards" were those applicable to new light-duty vehicles that EPA had initially proposed for motorcycles starting in 1980.

The follow-on standards adopted by the agency established a level of twelve grams per kilometer for carbon monoxide and a flat five grams per kilometer for hydrocarbons.

The EPA noted that the more liberal 1980 emission standards would nevertheless result in a 54 percent reduction in hydrocarbons over an uncontrolled situation and a 49 percent reduction in carbon monoxide. The agency made it clear that it may propose more stringent controls in the future if air quality needs dictate such a course of action or if the cost-effectiveness relationships between motorcycles and various other sources of air pollution change.

10

Water Pollution Controls for the Iron and Steel Industry

Robert L. Greene

Under the provisions of the Federal Water Pollution Control Act Amendments of 1970, the Environmental Protection Agency (EPA) was required to establish performance standards, by industry, for the discharge of pollutants into the navigable waters of the United States. The amendments required that by July 1, 1977, each industry reduce the discharge of pollutants to levels achievable with the "best practical technology" (BPT). By July 1, 1983, each industry was required to reduce discharges further to levels consistent with the use of the "best available technology" (BAT). These standards were to bring about "reasonable progress" toward the national goal of eliminating the discharge of all pollutants.

On March 29, 1976, EPA proposed regulations that would impose progressively stricter standards concerning the quantity and quality of water effluents discharged by the iron and steel manufacturing industry.[1] In order to meet these standards, individual firms may have to install control technology such as settling ponds if land is available, elaborate filtration systems for water discharges, and more water recycling equipment in some hot forming processes. All plants, however, will not have to install all such equipment. The specific control technology to be used is left to the individual plant because the standards are based on pounds of effluent per ton of product. Moreover, the control technology that will be needed depends on specific

---

This chapter is edited from "Effluent Guidelines and Standards for Existing and New Sources in the Iron and Steel Manufacturing Point Source Category: 40 C.F.R. 420," Comments of the Council on Wage and Price Stability before the Environmental Protection Agency, June 24, 1976.

[1] 41 Fed. Reg. 12990 (March 29, 1976).

operations of each plant and the degree of control already attained at each plant.

Background

The EPA has prepared an assessment of the inflationary impact of the proposed regulations.[2] Because of the lead time required for construction and installation of control apparatus, the agency has based its estimates of the aggregate economic impacts of the proposed regulation on an assumed BPT compliance date of July 1, 1979 (rather than the legally established date of July 1, 1977), and an assumed BAT compliance date of July 1, 1983.

This study is prompted by two principal concerns: first, EPA's analysis of the inflationary impact of the proposals has certain shortcomings; and second, the regulations themselves contain possible inefficiencies. It is important that EPA consider—to the maximum extent permitted by the Federal Water Pollution Control Act—the economic impact of these proposals and ultimately promulgate standards that are the most cost-effective means of achieving improved water quality. It is equally important that EPA complete a thorough analysis of the economic impact of its proposals so that the Congress and the public can be fully informed of the costs and benefits to the economy resulting from the effluent guidelines.

In its inflationary impact assessment, EPA projects that between 1975 and 1983 the iron and steel manufacturing industry will incur total capital costs of about $2.48 billion to meet the BPT and BAT guidelines as well as standards of performance proposed for new plants.[3] During the same nine-year period, the aggregated annual operating and maintenance costs associated with meeting these standards will total about $1.30 billion[4]

In view of the magnitude of these costs, the proposed regulations

---

[2] Environmental Protection Agency, *Economic Analysis of Proposed and Interim Final Effluent Guidelines: Integrated Iron and Steel Industry*, EPA-230/1-76-048 (March 1976), p. 9-1; hereinafter referred to as *Integrated Steel Economic Analysis*. See also Environmental Protection Agency, *Economic Analysis of Proposed and Interim Final Effluent Guidelines: The Specialty Steel Industry*, EPA-230/1-74-034A (February 1976); hereinafter referred to as *Specialty Steel Economic Analysis*.

[3] *Integrated Steel Economic Analysis*, p. 9-2. The estimate of $2.48 billion was derived by taking the EPA estimate of $2.31 billion, which represents the costs to the carbon steel producers that account for 93 percent of the total domestic shipments of all steel products, and dividing by 0.93 to yield an estimate of costs to the entire industry. All subsequent aggregate estimates include this adjustment unless otherwise noted.

[4] Ibid., p. 9-3.

could have an adverse effect on inflation in the United States if the economic benefits of improved water quality are less than the costs. On the other hand, if the benefits are greater than the costs, the guidelines will contribute to greater economic efficiency and will reduce inflationary pressures.[5] In order to make such determinations, the benefits must be put into terms that are more meaningful than tons of pollutants removed from the environment. Therefore, EPA should further assess the benefits in a manner outlined in this study.

It is equally important that the objectives of these guidelines be achieved in the least costly manner. In the course of this study, the data presented in the EPA technical documents and other data submitted by EPA have been reviewed.[6] This review has raised questions about the cost-effectiveness of the guidelines. Therefore, EPA is urged to evaluate the observations in this study; if they are correct, EPA should reevaluate and adjust the standards, to the extent possible or feasible, to achieve greater cost-effectiveness.

Four aspects of the proposed regulations are worthy of intensive review and possible modification. First, there is the issue of trading off short-term benefits in order to secure long-term savings, with no sacrifice in the long-term benefits. For example, it would appear worthwhile to explore the possibility of setting less stringent 1977 (BPT) standards as a means of reducing significantly the costs of attaining the water quality improvements implicit in the more stringent 1983 (BAT) standards.

Second, as in so many issues of this type, the additional costs of realizing the improvements implied by the stricter 1983 (BAT) standards appear to be disproportionately high. This study questions whether attaining the final few percentage points of reduction in effluents is worth the additional cost.

Third, EPA should investigate whether improved water quality might be achieved at less cost by adopting slightly less stringent standards for some industries and making up the difference by promulgating tighter standards for other industries. In other words, the total social cost of reaching any given level of water quality

---

[5] Because benefits such as the value of cleaner water are not included in price indexes, these anti-inflationary effects will not show up fully in measures such as the consumer price index. Nevertheless, when benefits to society exceed costs to society, the real effect is anti-inflationary.

[6] Environmental Protection Agency, *Development Document for Interim Final Effluent Limitation Guidelines and Proposed New Source Performance Standards for Forming, Finishing and Specialty Steel Segments of the Iron and Steel Manufacturing Point Source Category*, EPA 440/1-76-048-b, 2 vols. (March 1976); hereinafter referred to as *Development Document*.

could be reduced by tightening standards for those industries in which the marginal cost of pollution abatement is low and relaxing standards for those in which the marginal cost is high.

Finally, the proposed standards contain several subcategories that pertain to specific manufacturing processes, and the marginal costs of pollution abatement appear to vary widely among them. If this analysis is correct, then the cost of achieving any given level of pollution abatement in the iron and steel industry would be reduced by tightening requirements for those processes in which the marginal cost is low and relaxing requirements for those processes in which the marginal cost is high.

The iron and steel industry is a key component of the U.S. economy. It constitutes nearly 3 percent of total gross national product, and iron and steel are basic raw materials that appear in products U.S. consumers use every day. Thus, the potential impact of the proposed standards upon the national economy is extremely large, and their ramifications should be carefully examined before the regulation is implemented.

EPA's Inflation Impact Assessment

In this section the more significant conclusions of EPA's analysis of the inflationary impact of the proposed guidelines are set forth. The conclusions regarding costs will be noted first, followed by those regarding benefits.

Costs. EPA has quantified the substantial costs that would result from these guidelines:[7]

- Between 1975 and 1977, incremental capital expenditures required to meet these guidelines will total about $1.43 billion, of which about 90 percent, or $1.29 billion, will be associated with the BPT guidelines.

- Between 1975 and 1983, total incremental capital costs related to these guidelines will total about $2.48 billion.

- Between 1975 and 1977, incremental operating and maintenance costs will total about $0.13 billion, all of which will be attributable to the BPT guidelines.

---

[7] See *Integrated Steel Economic Analysis*, pp. 9-2, 9-3, and 9-5. These estimates incorporate the relief afforded the Mahoning River Valley Region. For details, see 41 Fed. Reg. 12994.

- Between 1975 and 1983, incremental operating and maintenance costs will total about $1.30 billion.

- The capital expenditures and operating and maintenance expenses required to meet these guidelines will increase the 1977 average price of steel by $2.44 a ton, which represents an increase of less than 1 percent over the baseline forecast—an estimate used to measure the economic impact.[8]

- By 1983, the average price increase is expected to be about $4.69 a ton, or about 1.3 percent over the baseline price.[9]

- The energy requirements associated with the guidelines will increase by about 30 trillion British thermal units (Btu) in the short run (1975–1977) and 270 trillion Btu in the long run (1975–1983)—about 1 percent of the total energy requirements for iron and steel production.

Several costs were not included in determining the impact of the guidelines: the costs of land acquisition; the costs of site clearance (such as relocating existing plant equipment); various costs of interconnecting utility runs between the treatment facilities, battery limits, and process equipment areas; and costs of expanding support utilities such as sewage facilities, river water pumping stations, and boiler capacity.[10] Although these costs might be relatively small when compared with the total, some indication of their magnitude should be included in the estimate of total costs. If the inclusion of these costs would contribute nothing to the analysis, EPA should state this point.

Benefits. An inflationary impact analysis should evaluate and, to the extent possible, quantify the benefits of a proposal as well as its

---

[8] These estimates from EPA's economic impact analysis (*Integrated Steel Economic Analysis*) differ from those cited at 41 Fed. Reg. 13001. As stated in the *Federal Register* notice, total capital costs by 1983 will be about $2.03 billion, of which $1.31 billion will be BPT costs and $0.72 billion will be BAT costs. Annual operating and maintenance costs by 1983 will be about $365 million, of which $201 million will be BPT costs and $164 million will be BAT costs. There are several reasons for these differences: the economic impact analysis is based on 1983 capacity, whereas the *Federal Register* estimates are based on 1972 production levels; in addition, the economic impact analysis recognizes economies of scale and includes construction in progress, whereas the *Federal Register* estimates do not. This study therefore has relied on the estimates used in EPA's economic impact analysis.

[9] All these estimates are the incremental costs of these guidelines only and do not include the costs of control equipment already in place. For example, if all costs are included, the price increase is projected to be $9.60 a ton by 1983.

[10] *Development Document*, vol. 2, p. 526.

costs. The EPA analysis does discuss the types of pollutants that are discharged into water by iron and steel manufacturing operations.[11] It also provides estimates of the percentage reduction in pollutants discharged by the iron and steel industry that would result from implementing the guidelines. The analysis does not, however, estimate the extent to which the proposals would contribute to improvements in aggregate water quality. (Improvement in water quality is a more meaningful measure of benefits than tons of pollutants removed, especially with respect to the incremental reductions obtained by moving from BPT to BAT.) Nor does the analysis attempt to give dollar values to any of these benefits so that they can be compared with the costs incurred.

Such a benefit analysis, including a comparison of the benefits and the costs incurred by the proposals, is needed so that the Congress and the public can review the economic impact of the proposals. Indeed, if the inflationary impact of the proposals is to be properly assessed, the comparison of benefits and costs must be made.

Further analysis of benefits is also relevant to EPA's determination of what standards to promulgate under the Federal Water Pollution Act. For example, in promulgating BPT standards to be achieved by July 1, 1977, EPA is expressly directed by section 304(b)(1)(B) of the act to consider "the total cost of application of technology *in relation to the effluent reduction benefits to be achieved* from such application" (emphasis added). Further, the BAT standards to be promulgated for July 1, 1983, are directed by the act to be "economically achievable" and to require "reasonable further progress" toward pollutant-free water.

In some instances, it may be difficult to measure the economic value of the benefits. In these instances, surrogates, such as miles of waterfront made available for recreation, could be used in lieu of quantified economic estimates. If such surrogates could be identified and estimated, the economic analysis would be improved. Although the precise inflationary (or deflationary) impact still could not be stated, the use of such surrogate variables would make possible a more meaningful analysis of cost-effectiveness. That is, calculations could be made to show the cost per unit of improvement, such as the cost per additional mile of improved waterfront. It could then be determined whether the costs of achieving the objective (that is, the social benefits of cleaner water) are minimized, particularly when these

---

[11] Examples include cyanide, sulfuric acid, phenol, zinc, oil and grease, and suspended solids.

per-unit costs are compared with costs of alternative methods of reaching the same objective.

EPA should delineate more specifically the contributions these guidelines would make toward improved water quality. The nature of the pollution problem in the waters affected by the iron and steel industry needs to be discussed, and the extent to which the iron and steel industry contributes to this problem should be estimated. Finally, since EPA does provide estimates of the percentage reduction in pollutants discharged by the iron and steel industry that would result from implementation of the guidelines, the agency should also determine the extent to which the proposed guidelines would contribute to improvements in the aggregate U.S. water quality. Such a statistic would be of greater value to the general public than EPA's present use of tons of pollutants removed from the environment, and it is the general public that must ultimately bear the cost of the proposed guidelines through higher prices for products.

Concerns with the Standards

This study assumes that, once the proposed iron and steel guidelines are implemented, there will be improvements in the quality of affected waters. Nonetheless, it is still important to estimate whether the proposals are the most cost-effective (least costly) way to attain those improvements. This analysis is important both to EPA's final decision about the proposed standards and to the Congress's and the public's oversight of the Federal Water Pollution Control Act. Therefore, EPA is urged to reconsider certain aspects of the proposed guidelines and to make appropriate adjustments, if necessary.

Regulation by Manufacturing Process. One possible adjustment to the proposed standards would be to set different levels of effluent control for individual production processes. EPA has completed significant economic analyses showing that different control levels will achieve different levels of effluent reduction. These analyses identify the projected industrywide capital costs associated with the different control levels, the discharges of total suspended solids (TSS) and oil and grease (OG) associated with each alternative control level, and the alternative percentage reductions in discharges of TSS and OG that will be attained. EPA has not, however, presented any analysis of the cost-effectiveness of alternative control strategies that might be used to attain the same improvements in water quality that are associated with the effluent control levels that EPA has promulgated for BPT and proposed for BAT.

137

This study has analyzed five processes in iron and steel operations with effluent discharges that involve heavy waste loads of TSS. These are: (1) hot forming primary with scarfing, (2) hot forming primary without scarfing, (3) hot forming hot strip sheet, (4) hot forming section, and (5) integrated seamless pipes and tubes. In the course of analyzing EPA's technical data, this study found a wide divergence in the costs associated with removing a ton of TSS. For example, at the 1983 BAT control level, the incremental annual costs (that is, the added costs of gains from BPT to BAT) per ton of TSS removed range from about $1,957 for the hot forming primary with scarfing process to about $18,000 per ton of TSS removed for the integrated seamless pipes and tubes subcategory.[12] The intermediate values are about $3,600 a ton for the hot forming primary without scarfing process, about $4,200 a ton for the hot forming hot strip sheet process, and about $10,170 a ton for the hot forming section process. With the exception of the hot forming with and without scarfing processes, the proposed guidelines for these subcategories require zero discharge at the BAT control level.[13]

The preceding numbers overestimate the costs of reducing TSS because it is assumed that all the process costs are attributable to the removal of TSS; part of the control costs are in fact related to the removal of OG. Thus, the control costs are common, in part, to both pollutants. The analysis presented below blurs this distinction for reasons of exposition. EPA should consider these problems of "jointness" in its analysis of cost-effectiveness. The importance of these estimates is not their absolute values but rather their relative values. Comparisons between values are valid for the reason that, with the exception of the hot forming primary process and the hot forming flat plate process, the relationship in these subcategories between the pounds of TSS and the pounds of OG is relatively stable (about 2.5–3.5 to 1).

In order to minimize the total cost of meeting any given level of pollution reduction (that is, to achieve cost-effectiveness), the incremental cost per ton of TSS removed for each subcategory should be equated as nearly as possible to the cost per ton of TSS removed

---

[12] The EPA data that provide the bases for these calculations presume that treatment will take place at the end of each process. Some firms, however, will be able to lower costs by commingling the discharges from several processes at a central treatment point.

[13] For purposes of analytical discussion, these comments are restricted to five processes whose principal effluents are TSS and OG. The implications of these comments, however, extend to all the subcategories and should not be interpreted as applying only to these five.

for every other subcategory. In light of this criterion and the marginal BAT cost discrepancies among the processes mentioned above, the question arises whether cost-effective guidelines are being proposed. For some processes (such as integrated pipes and tubes and hot forming sections), in which the BAT-prescribed limit is zero discharge, the incremental annual compliance costs per ton are far higher than the incremental annual costs per ton for other processes (such as hot forming primary with and without scarfing), in which the allowable discharge level is greater than zero. Thus, EPA should consider the desirability and the feasibility of tightening the discharge limits of those subcategories with relatively low compliance costs per ton and relaxing the limits on those subcategories with relatively high compliance costs per ton.[14]

Such adjustments would lower the total costs of the same amount of pollutant removal. For example, if the BAT level of effluent control for the integrated seamless pipes and tubes subcategory is relaxed so that one (rather than the proposed zero) ton of TSS can be discharged, the cost saving would be about $18,000. If the BAT effluent control level for the hot forming primary with scarfing subcategory were stiffened to achieve the removal of one additional ton of TSS, the increase in cost would be about $2,000. The net effect would be to remove the same quantity of tons of TSS, but the total costs would be reduced by about $16,000 (that is, $18,000 minus $2,000).

Costliness of BAT. Although the Federal Water Pollution Control Act appears to require that the 1983 BAT standards be stricter than the 1977 BPT standards, it still requires that the 1983 standards be "economically achievable" and "reasonable." This study has analyzed data submitted by EPA and questions the economic efficiency of the proposed BAT standards. That is, are the incremental benefits of reaching the BAT standard worth the incremental costs?

Two subcategories—the integrated seamless pipes and tubes and the hot forming section—illustrate the need for further analysis of this issue. At a model plant, the incremental BAT cost (that is, the added costs of going from BPT to BAT) per ton of TSS removed for the seamless pipes and tubes subcategory is projected to be about $18,000 annually at the BAT limit of zero discharge, and the incremental reduction in TSS over BPT is about five tons a year. At the final step of the BPT standard, however, the incremental costs per ton are about $1,000 annually with the removal of about thirty-four

---

[14] Again, the concern is with minimizing the cost of meeting a given objective, *not* whether this objective is the most appropriate one.

tons a year. According to EPA data, the BPT guidelines will achieve about a 95 percent reduction in TSS discharges, and the BAT guidelines will achieve a 100 percent reduction. In the hot forming section subcategory, the incremental cost per ton of TSS removed at BAT is about $10,170 annually per plant. The benefits will be the elimination of an additional thirty-seven tons of TSS annually as the BAT limit of zero discharge is reached. At the last incremental step of BPT control, the annual cost per ton of TSS removed is about $630, and the benefit is the elimination of about 195 tons of TSS annually. EPA data indicate that the level of TSS control attained by the BPT guidelines in this subcategory will be about 94.7 percent, whereas the BAT guidelines will achieve 100 percent of TSS control.

These two examples are representative of the concern about whether the incremental benefits warrant the incremental costs. In the case of the integrated seamless pipes and tubes subcategory, are the benefits of removing five additional tons of TSS a year worth having an average plant spend about $18,000 annually per ton, or a total of about $90,000 annually? That is, are the economic benefits of moving from 95 percent control at BPT to 100 percent control at BAT worth the incremental costs? The same question can be asked in the case of all the subcategories. EPA should reevaluate its technical assessment of the incremental benefits and incremental costs of the BAT guidelines relative to the BPT guidelines. In the process, the agency should provide greater economic or technical rationale for some of the more strict BAT subcategory guidelines, particularly when the BAT costs per ton are high relative to the BPT costs.

Modification of BPT. EPA should also reevaluate whether the promulgated BPT standards are the most efficient interim step toward meeting whatever 1983 standards are adopted. Such reconsideration would involve evaluating a possible trade-off between, on the one hand, possible long-term permanent cost savings (by the imposition of less strict BPT controls) and, on the other hand, reduced short-run pollution control that would not sacrifice the long-run 1983 goals.

Table 10–1 summarizes technical data submitted by EPA to the Council on Wage and Price Stability. For the iron and steel industry as a whole, conformity with the promulgated BPT standards would result in a reduction to 45,000 tons of TSS annually (a 98.6 percent control) for a capital outlay of $1.211 billion.[15] Going from promulgated BPT standards to proposed BAT standards would result in an

---

[15] These aggregate capital costs do not include the 0.93 adjustment referred to earlier.

TABLE 10–1

Comparison of Two 1977 "Best Practical Technology" (BPT) Standards as Interim Standards Preceding 1983 "Best Available Technology" (BAT) Standards

	Incremental Capital Costs (millions of dollars) (1)	Discharge of TSS after Standards (thousands of tons annually) (2)	Net Reduction of TSS Discharge (thousands of tons annually) (3)	Level of Control Achieved as a Percent of Raw Waste Load[a] (percent) (4)
From raw waste load to promulgated BPT standards[a]	1,211	45.0	3,270.0[b]	98.6[c]
From raw waste load to alternative (less stringent) BPT standards	995	118.0	3,197.0[b]	96.4[c]
From promulgated BPT standards to proposed BAT standards	674	3.4	41.6[d]	99.9[e]
From alternative (less stringent) BPT standards to proposed BAT standards	684	3.4	114.6[d]	99.9[e]

[a] Raw waste load is the effluent discharge of total suspended solids (TSS) in the absence of any control technology. This waste load is assumed to be 3,315,000 tons annually.

[b] Net reductions are calculated by subtracting discharges after the standards (column [2]) from 3,315,000.

[c] Calculated by dividing raw waste load (3,315,000) into net reduction shown in column (3).

[d] Calculated by subtracting the BAT control level of 3,400 tons from the relevant BPT control level. These numbers show the incremental improvement in discharges associated with the BAT level over and above the indicated BPT level.

[e] Calculated by subtracting 3,400 tons from 3,315,000 tons and dividing the difference by 3,315,000 tons.

Source: Technical data submitted by the Environmental Protection Agency to the Council on Wage and Price Stability.

additional reduction to 3,400 tons of TSS annually (a 99.9 percent control), for an incremental capital outlay of about $674 million. If the level of BPT control is relaxed incrementally to a less strict control level (alternative BPT in Table 10–1), however, TSS discharges would be reduced to 118,000 tons annually (a 96.4 percent control), for a capital outlay of about $995 million. Moreover, going from the alternative BPT to the proposed BAT—the same 1983 level as the level attained under the promulgated BPT control level—would result in a reduction of TSS discharges to 3,400 tons annually (a 99.9 percent control), for an incremental capital outlay of $684 million.

The net saving in capital costs as a result of going to the 1983 BAT control level from the present control level via the alternative BPT control level is about $206 million.[16] The implication of this saving is that TSS discharges will be greater during the short term by about 73,000 tons annually.[17] Since the 1983 goals are the same, the only sacrifice is in the level of control during the 1977–1983 period. Moreover, the short-run loss in control probably will be less because EPA does not expect the BPT control technologies to be in place until sometime between 1979 and 1981.

Thus, the question can be raised whether the 73,000 tons of TSS annually that could be eliminated for a period of two to four years is worth a capital outlay of $206 million. In order to achieve both economic efficiency and good public policy, it is necessary to weigh such trade-offs between pollution abatement objectives and the cost of reaching those objectives. This type of analysis is particularly important when the only sacrifice involves short-run objectives while the long-run goal remains intact. In the example above, $206 million could be saved forever at a loss of 73,000 tons of TSS

---

[16] The difference in the BPT control levels is a saving in BPT capital costs of $216 million (that is, $1,211 million minus $995 million). The incremental capital cost of going to BAT from the alternative BPT control level is increased by $10 million (that is, $684 million minus $674 million). Thus, the net saving in capital costs by 1983 associated with the alternative BPT control level is $206 million (that is, $216 million minus $10 million). According to the EPA staff, the saving is attributable to the use of filters that are necessary to reach the promulgated BPT control level but will not be required once recycling is installed to achieve the BAT level of zero discharge. This position differs somewhat from the industry position, which argues that filters will also be required to remove impurities built up during recycling. This study has accepted EPA's technological assessment.

[17] The promulgated BPT control level reduces TSS discharges to 45,000 tons annually. The alternative BPT control level allows additional discharges of TSS of 73,000 tons annually (that is, 118,000 minus 45,000). In both cases the BAT level of control will be discharges totaling about 3,400 tons annually—a reduction of about 3.312 million tons.

annually being introduced into the nation's navigable waters for a period of about three years. EPA should further evaluate the position that a short-run incremental improvement in water quality is worth this cost. Only when such evaluations are made will it be possible to assess the inflationary (deflationary) impact of the guidelines.

Regulation of Other Industries. Finally, EPA should make a cost-effectiveness analysis that compares the iron and steel industry with other industries that have common effluents. For example, there is no comparison of the costs per ton of TSS (or other effluents) removed from the iron and steel industry's discharges with the costs per ton of TSS that might be removed from the waste streams of other types of plants (either municipal or industrial) that are discharging similar pollutants into the same water. If such an analysis were completed, it might be shown that the same amount of pollutants (common to both plants) could be removed at a lower cost by relaxing (tightening) the guidelines on the iron and steel industry and tightening (relaxing) the guidelines for other industries. In this event, the total costs of cleaning up the affected waters to any given level could be reduced. EPA should devote more effort to this type of integrated analysis in establishing future effluent guidelines for particular industries.

Summary and Conclusions

This study has commented on EPA's inflationary impact assessment of the iron and steel effluent guidelines and on four possible inefficiencies in the regulations themselves. Although this analysis has been limited to discharges of total suspended solids, the points that have been discussed have broader application to all the effluents that will be controlled by the guidelines. This study does not question the position that there will be water quality benefits associated with both the BPT guidelines and the BAT guidelines. In order to make an assessment of the inflationary impact of the guidelines, however, EPA must define benefits in terms other than tons of pollutants removed.

Since it is not always possible to quantify economic benefits, it is difficult to measure the precise inflationary impact of the regulations. Nevertheless, a cost-effectiveness analysis of a given regulatory objective can be completed by using surrogates, such as the tons of pollutants removed. Cost-effectiveness analysis facilitates the determination of whether an objective is being attained in the least costly manner. This study has found a significant variance in the costs per ton of TSS removed between subcategories of the iron and steel industry, particularly at the BAT control level. In view of these findings, EPA is urged to evaluate the guidelines to determine if a more cost-effective set of alternative control levels by subcategories exists. In addition, EPA is urged to compare the BAT costs to the iron and steel industry for a ton of effluent removed with the BAT costs per ton removed for other industries with common effluents. Such a comparison would facilitate a determination of whether the most cost-effective combination of interindustry guidelines is being implemented.

EPA is also urged to complete further evaluation of proposed BAT control levels in view of the significantly higher costs for effluents removed at the BAT control levels (as indicated by the costs per ton of TSS) relative to the costs per ton at the BPT control levels. The question is raised whether the benefits are commensurate with the increased costs.

Finally, EPA is urged to complete further economic evaluation of the BPT control levels it has promulgated as interim final guidelines. Based on the technical data EPA submitted for analysis, there appears to be some possibility for cost savings with relatively small sacrifices in short-run improvement of water quality by relaxing some of the BPT subcategory limitations. If such revisions are not possible, EPA should provide more technical and economic data in support of the BPT standards that are promulgated.

Only when further evaluations such as those suggested above are completed can economically sound and noninflationary or minimally inflationary guidelines be established.

Under provisions of the 1977 amendments to the Federal Water Pollution Control Act, the attainment of BAT standards has been moved to 1984. Moreover, the control level of conventional pollutants, such as total suspended solids (TSS) and oil and grease (OG), has been changed to one achievable by July 1, 1984, through the application of the "best conventional pollutant control technology" (BCT). There is a limitation that the cost cannot exceed the cost for pretreatment of those effluents discharged into publicly owned treatment works. The 1984 BAT standards, which are stricter than the BCT standards, were retained for toxic pollutants. All other pollutants must be reduced to EPA-determined levels no later than July 1, 1987.

In September 1977, on an appeal by the American Iron and Steel Institute and its individual members, the Third District Court of

Appeals remanded the 1977 BPT Phase II water effluent guidelines. The bases for the remand included: (1) the failure of the agency adequately to consider site specific costs (such as land costs), (2) the failure adequately to evaluate age as a variable determining the cost and feasibility of retrofitting, and (3) an unclear record about whether the administrator was apprised of the true economic impacts of the regulations. In addition, an agreement (consent order) was signed with the National Resources Defense Council that requires EPA to reevaluate the 1983 (now 1984) BAT standards for toxic pollutants. This agreement could result in even more stringent BAT standards.

At present, EPA is preparing to propose a new set of BPT and BCT/BAT standards. That proposal is expected in late 1979.

11

Reducing Airport Noise

John F. Morrall III

Airport noise has created major controversy since 1958 when the first commercial jets were introduced in the United States, perhaps peaking with the introduction of the Concorde supersonic aircraft. The Federal Aviation Administration and the Environmental Protection Agency, as well as state and local governments, have all rushed in with regulations, curfews, and other governmental interventions in an attempt to quiet airport noise. But a practical and relatively simple solution requiring minimum governmental intervention may have been overlooked. This chapter presents such an approach.

This study recommends that the Federal Aviation Administration (FAA) study the possibility of developing a tax-incentive approach to the problem of reducing aircraft noise as an alternative to present and proposed regulatory schemes. Adoption of a nationwide tax-incentive approach would require statutory enactment by the Congress. A study of these issues by the FAA would seem appropriate, however, in light of the broad view that the FAA has taken of the problem of aircraft noise.[1]

A tax-incentive approach would be potentially simpler and more

---

This chapter is edited from John F. Morrall III, "A Proposal to Reduce Airport Noise Through the Application of a Decibel Charge," April 1976. Although the author was an economist with the Council on Wage and Price Stability when this paper was written, the views expressed are those of the author but not necessarily those of the council.

[1] The FAA may choose to conduct such a study in cooperation with the Environmental Protection Agency (EPA). Alternatively, the secretary of transportation may choose to conduct such a study under the authority of 49 U.S.C., section 1354(e), the powers of which were transferred to the secretary by 49 U.S.C., section 1655(c).

cost-effective than the detailed and complicated existing noise standards. Moreover, it appears feasible to implement a tax-incentive approach to aircraft noise because of the relatively small number of emission sources and the already developed techniques of measurement.

Regulatory initiatives in the area of aircraft noise abatement policy have proliferated over the past year. The FAA has proposed regulations requiring retrofit of noisy aircraft and a two-segment landing approach.[2] In the former case the estimated costs exceed the estimated benefits, whereas in the latter case the benefits would likely exceed the costs.[3] In addition to these proposed methods of reducing aircraft noise, the FAA has prescribed detailed noise limits for new aircraft in Federal Aviation Regulation, Part 36 (FAR 36),[4] and has considered other methods such as the refan proposal and various takeoff and landing procedures.

The Environmental Protection Agency (EPA) has also proposed various regulations to abate aircraft noise in eight areas: takeoff, approach, minimum altitudes, retrofit for large turbojets, type certification for supersonic civil aircraft, tightening of FAR 36, type certification for new propeller-driven small airplanes, and noise standards for short-haul aircraft.[5]

In a recent announcement for public comment on airport noise policy, the FAA noted four possible restrictions on airport use that might be imposed either individually or in combination: curfews, a total ban on jet-powered aircraft, a ban or curfew on all aircraft that do not meet FAR 36 criteria for noise levels, and a limit on the number of operations.[6]

There is a strong possibility that promulgation of this multitude of detailed aircraft noise regulations may not be the least costly way

---

[2] For an analysis of the cost and benefits of these proposals, see Council on Wage and Price Stability, "Comments of the Council on Wage and Price Stability Regarding Proposed Aircraft Noise Retrofit Requirements," CWPS-38 (April 7, 1975); and "Comments of the Council on Wage and Price Stability on EPA Proposal to Reduce Noise Level Surrounding Airports," CWPS-109 (November 28, 1975).

[3] This conclusion of the CWPS was qualified to the extent that safety considerations penalized the two-segment landing approach. The council was not able to quantify the safety factor.

[4] See "Noise Standards: Aircraft Type Certification; Federal Aviation Regulations Part 36," 34 Fed. Reg. 18364 (November 18, 1969); "Noise Standards for Newly Produced Airplanes of Older Type Designs," 38 Fed. Reg. 29569 (October 26, 1973); and "Civil Aircraft Sonic Boom," 38 Fed. Reg. 8051 (March 28, 1973).

[5] For a summary of EPA's proposals, see Environmental Protection Agency, *Project Report: Noise Standards for Civil Subsonic Turbojet Engined Powered Airplane* (December 16, 1974), pp. 1-4 to 1-6.

[6] 40 Fed. Reg. 28845.

of achieving the desired level of noise abatement. The four FAA restrictions on airport use—as well as other proposed regulations— would affect existing equipment, pilot operating procedures, individual airport operating procedures, and even the development of new technology. The cost-effectiveness of such procedures for abating noise would depend upon thousands of variables, including the aircraft, the pilot, the airport, the time of day, the weather, and even the weight of the aircraft. If, however, pilots and the managers of the individual airports and airlines were given adequate incentives, they should be able to adjust operations to achieve noise abatement goals in a more cost-effective way. Hence, a program of incentives to individual decision makers is likely to be better than regulations for achieving noise reduction.

At present, airline management has little incentive to reduce aircraft noise. To the extent that the airline industry has attempted to reduce the social costs of noise, the effort has been mainly a by-product of complying with noise regulations. Moreover, despite the intent of the regulations, complying with them does not always effectively reduce noise. For example, the operating procedures used to meet the FAR 36 noise levels in the certifying tests are not usually used in actual operations, so that in practice FAR 36 noise levels are usually exceeded. A further difficulty is that enforcement of complex regulations is not always an easy process. The higher the cost of reducing noise, the greater the resistance of the airlines to noise reduction. This political reality may explain why regulation has up to now produced little noise relief.

The Pollution Tax Alternative

A better approach than regulation might be one in which airline management and airport operators had built-in incentives to minimize the noise impact presently borne by third parties. In technical language, this is known as internalizing the externality. Economists have long advocated doing this by a tax on pollution.[7] Although admin-

---

[7] For example, see the *Economic Report of the President, 1971*; Russell E. Train, chairman of the Council on Environmental Quality, address delivered at the Atlantic Council, Battelle Memorial Institute Conference, Washington, D.C., January 15, 1971; Charles L. Schultze and others, *Setting National Priorities: The 1972 Budget* (Washington, D.C.: Brookings Institution, 1971); Charles L. Schultze and others, *Setting National Priorities: The 1973 Budget* (Washington, D.C.: Brookings Institution, 1972); and Allen V. Kneese and Charles L. Schultze, *Pollution, Prices, and Public Policy* (Washington, D.C.: Brookings Institution, 1975).

This approach has also been recommended by the Organization for Economic

istrative costs and particular problems of measurement may make this method difficult to apply for some forms of pollution, this does not appear to be the case for aircraft noise pollution. The number of major airports is small,[8] and the state of the art of measuring aircraft noise around airports is highly developed—mainly because EPA and FAA have funded research. These two factors may make the application of effluent charges—or tax incentives—to the problem of aircraft noise both feasible and desirable.[9]

One advantage that standards (assuming perfect enforcement) sometimes have over effluent charges is that they are immediate and certain. Public health considerations do not appear to be as important for noise pollution, however, as for irreversible or unacceptable forms of pollution such as mercury, cadmium, and asbestos poisoning, because airport noise is mainly a nuisance.[10] The characteristics of the problem of abating aircraft noise appear to make it a particularly good test case for the effluent-charge approach to pollution abatement.

The advantage of the effluent-charge approach is that it forces management to count the costs of pollution to third parties in the same way it counts the costs of materials or labor. Just as management strives to reduce the inputs of labor and materials to the point at which their marginal contribution to the revenue of the firm equals their marginal cost, so should management strive to reduce the effluent charges and therefore pollution to the point at which further

Co-operation and Development and has been adopted for water pollution in both France and the Netherlands. See OECD, *The Polluter Pays Principle* (Paris, 1975), for a discussion of the pros and cons of this approach and its implementation in France and the Netherlands.

[8] Fifty-eight airports in the "major hubs" accounted for 68 percent of passenger enplanements in 1972. If the thirty-nine airports in "medium hubs" are added, 86 percent of total enplanements is accounted for. See Civil Aeronautics Board and U.S. Department of Transportation, *Airport Activity Statistics: 12 Months Ended December 31, 1972* (1973), Tables 3 and 4.

[9] The application of tax incentives to reduce aircraft noise has been proposed and discussed by R. Jackson, "Airport Noise and Congestion: A Peak Load Pricing Solution," *Applied Economics* (September 1971), pp. 197–203; Mahlon R. Straszheim, "Efficiency and Equity Considerations in the Financing of Noise Abatement Activities at Airports," *Rivista Internazionale D. Economonia Des Trasport* (April 1975), pp. 3–14; and A.A. Walters, *Noise and Prices* (London: Oxford University Press, 1975), pp. 116–44.

[10] EPA argues (but presents no evidence) that since some people living close to airports could suffer hearing or psychological damage, aircraft noise is a public health problem. The decline in noise levels over time, however, and the long period (twenty to forty years) it takes for hearing damage to develop under these conditions bring into question EPA's assertion. Nevertheless, this issue deserves further investigation in setting policy on airport noise. If the problem is real, the noise tax could be set high enough to eliminate any public health hazard.

pollution abatement would cost more to the firm than society gains from one more unit reduction. This result is achieved when the per-unit marginal effluent tax is set equal to the per-unit marginal cost to society of pollution.

In theory, a set of noise regulations could duplicate the optimal outcome of the tax-incentive approach. But these regulations would have to be so detailed, comprehensive, and continuously changing that, in practice, the system would be impossibly complex and expensive to administer. The delays and complexity of the existing and proposed regulations to abate aircraft noise support this view.

One purpose of this study is to discuss the advantages of a tax-incentive approach to the airport noise problem and to calculate some hypothetical tax rates based on the available data in order to illustrate the possible workings and incentives of such a system. Such an approach would likely abate noise to a given level at lowest possible costs and, unlike the alternative, would be anti-inflationary. This study does not advocate any specific tax rates nor the abolition of noise standards. It does recommend that such a system be seriously considered and studied by the FAA in developing future policy on airport noise control.

Measuring the Costs of Airport Noise

The tax-incentive approach starts by identifying the social costs of aircraft noise pollution and proceeds by creating tax incentives or penalties that reflect these social costs. By means of the profit motive, such taxes force those responsible for producing aircraft noise to consider these social costs in their day-to-day operations. The social cost of airport noise derives, for the most part, from the nuisance that has made living near airports undesirable and has therefore depressed property values. The lower property values reflect a loss to society because the quality of the property affected by the noise has been diminished. There are also benefits that should be considered. Most likely, the air transportation services are greater than they would be if noise standards were more strict.

If one could find two identical pieces of property, one affected by aircraft noise of a certain intensity and one not affected, society's evaluation of the decline in the worth of the property because of aircraft noise would be measured by the difference in the price of the land. If enough such cases could be found and if housing markets were competitive, one would have a reasonable expectation that this measurement truly reflected the social cost of aircraft noise. Because of the great number of individual buyers and sellers of housing and because of the size of the purchase (which induces most families to search out alternatives and to weigh decisions carefully), most economists agree that housing markets are relatively competitive. Recently developed regression techniques allow the comparison of a great number of housing units that are "identical" except for their varying exposure to aircraft noise. These statistical analyses, which have been performed for a number of years and for a variety of airports, measure the decline in worth of the properties because of aircraft noise, and hence the implicit price or benefit of a unit reduction in aircraft noise.

The best known measurement of aircraft noise, and the one used by FAA, is the noise exposure forecast (NEF), which takes into account the relative incidence and effect of nighttime flights. This measure is expressed as:

$$NEF = EPNL + 10 \log (Nd + 16.7 \, Nn) - 88$$

where EPNL is the effective perceived noise level adjusted for pure tones and duration of flyovers, Nd is the number of daytime flights (7:00 A.M. to 10:00 P.M.), and Nn is the number of nighttime flights (10:00 P.M. to 7:00 A.M.). The NEF system gives nighttime flights a little more than twelve times as much weight as daytime flights.

Estimates of the percentage decline in property values per unit increase in NEF have been completed for New York, Los Angeles, Dallas, Boston, Minneapolis, San Francisco, San Jose, and Washington, D.C., for various years by different authors.[11] Recently, two studies analyzed the previous work in the field and summarized the results. One study, by Jon Nelson, concluded that a noise depreciation rate of 0.5 percent per unit increase in NEF was the best point estimate.[12] The other study, by A.A. Walters, concluded that the noise depreciation index for the United States is between 0.4 and 0.7 percent

---

[11] See F.C. Emerson, "The Determinants of Residential Value with Special Reference to the Effects of Aircraft Nuisance and Other Environmental Features" (Ph.D. dissertation, University of Minnesota, 1969); P.K. Dygert, "Estimation of the Cost of Aircraft Noise to Residential Activities" (Ph.D. dissertation, University of Michigan, 1973); I. Price, "The Social Cost of Airport Noise as Measured by Rental Changes: The Case of Logan Airport" (Ph.D. dissertation, Boston University, 1974); J.P. Nelson, *The Effects of Mobile-Source Air and Noise Pollution on Residential Property Values* (U.S. Department of Transportation, Office of the Secretary, 1975); and I.K. Paik, "Measurement of Environmental Externality in Particular Reference to Noise" (Ph.D. dissertation, Georgetown University, 1972).

[12] Nelson, *The Effects of Mobile-Source Air and Noise Pollution*, pp. 8–12.

for noise measurement units approximately equivalent to NEF units.[13] An estimate of 0.5 percent will be assumed in the following calculations.

The example has been constructed using 1972 data because that is the only year for which hard data exist.[14] All studies for the years since 1972 have had to extrapolate population changes, airport noise changes, and price and cost changes. Furthermore, the most recent property depreciation indexes per NEF are based on 1970 census data. The biases that exist because 1976 data are not available may very well cancel out. Before any system of tax incentives is implemented, further empirical work of this nature should be completed.

Using a 0.5 percent depreciation rate per NEF and EPA's estimate of the number of people living in 1972 within the NEF contours (between thirty and forty-five NEF at five NEF intervals), this study estimates the total cost of aircraft noise at $1.457 billion.[15] This procedure counts everyone living within the thirty to thirty-five NEF noise contour as experiencing 2.5 NEF noise depreciation units, everyone living within the thirty-five to forty NEF contour as experiencing 7.5 NEF noise depreciation units, and everyone living within the forty to forty-five NEF contour as experiencing 12.5 NEF noise depreciation units.

Calculations of Noise Taxes

In calculating the noise tax, this study uses a 10 percent social rate of discount.[16] This implies that property "rents" have been depressed because of airport noise by $145.7 million a year.[17] Since there were

---

[13] Walters, *Noise and Prices*, p. 105.

[14] The basis for most estimates of NEF noise levels and affected land and population is U.S. Department of Transportation, *Aircraft Noise Reduction Forecast*, vol. 1, *Summary Report for 23 Airports*, DOT-TST-75-3 (October 1974).

[15] These calculations are shown in the appendix to this study. EPA's estimates of the number of people affected by various noise levels exceed FAA's by almost 25 percent. EPA's estimates have been used.

[16] The social rate of discount is the interest rate at which public investment should be evaluated. There is no single "correct" rate, but 10 percent has often been used. It is important that different public investment projects be calculated at the same rate.

[17] Property values may be thought of as the capitalized value of the flow of services of the land. "Rent" is the per-year dollar value of that flow of services. If 10 percent is the prevalent interest rate for society, property "rents" may be estimated by the formula $R = (PV)i$, where PV equals the present value of the property, i equals the interest rate, and R equals the rent. The implicit assumption in this is that the rate is a perpetual stream of income.

approximately 10 million landings and takeoffs by commercial air-craft in the United States in 1972, the average noise cost per opera-tion would be $14.57. Levying a tax of this amount per aircraft landing or takeoff would have only a small effect in reducing noise pollution because there would be no benefits to an individual airline in reducing noise. If, instead of a fixed landing fee, the fine per operation were to vary by the contribution of the operation to the NEF level around the particular airport in question, weighted by the amount of population and property values within the various NEF contours around each airport, the reduction in noise pollution would be much greater.

It would be a simple procedure, for example, to record effective perceived noise level (EPNL) per takeoff and landing, note the time of day, and—from schedules developed for each airport based on NEF contour profiles and demographic data—calculate the tax per aircraft operation. Under this system, not only would the full damage to the environment from noise pollution be borne by the polluters, but incentives would be created that would lead to a reduction in noise to the optimal level, and this would be accomplished in the most efficient (least costly) manner.

The first effect of the tax would be a reducton in the amount of air service, if it is assumed that the tax paid by the airlines would be passed on to consumers.[18] Since the yearly tax would be about $146 million and total operating revenues of U.S. scheduled airlines was $11,163 million in 1972, the tax would be only about 1.3 percent of total revenues. And since the elasticity of the demand for air travel ranges from the Civil Aeronautics Board's estimate of −0.7 to several academicians' estimates of −2.0, the reduction in air service would be only about 1.0 to 2.6 percent in the first instance and less as air-lines reduced their taxes by adopting noise abatement procedures.[19]

---

[18] The Civil Aeronautics Board would have to grant fare increases that reflected the airlines' increased tax burden in order for this to occur. If the tax were not passed on, airline service would still be reduced, but by a different percentage than calculated in the text.

[19] For estimates of the elasticity of the demand for air travel, see Arthur S. DeVany, "The Revealed Value of Time in Air Travel," *Review of Economics and Statistics* (February 1974), pp. 77–82; and Phillip K. Verleger, "Models of the Demand for Air Transportation," *Bell Journal of Economics and Management Science* (Autumn 1972), pp. 437–52.

The estimate of reduction in air service assumes that the elasticity of demand for air travel does not vary with the amount of aircraft noise generated. Also, the reduction in air service for a given reduction in noise should be less under the tax-incentive approach than under the standards approach. This is because of the likely greater cost-effectiveness of the noise-tax approach.

There would be incentives to adopt landing and takeoff procedures (within FAA regulations) that reduced noise, to modify equipment to reduce noise, to retire noisy planes or operate them less, to operate at airports where less population would be affected, and to operate during the day rather than during the night.

The magnitude of some of these incentives can be easily calculated. For example, if nighttime operations account for 7.7 percent of the 10 million operations (sum of departures and arrivals), the average tax for a nighttime operation would be $94.73 compared with $7.89 for an otherwise identical daytime operation.[20] This difference in taxes represents a strong incentive to reduce the late-night operations, which are more disturbing than daytime operations.

Taxes also would vary by airport because the number of people affected by noise around different airports varies. From estimates of the number of people residing within the thirty NEF contours around certain airports and the relative traffic at each airport, an average tax per operation by airport can be calculated.[21] For example, at La Guardia Airport in New York, the average tax would be $84.61 per operation, whereas at Atlanta the tax would be only $6.02.[22] It is likely that at some—in fact most—of the airports in the United States the tax would be near zero. A cost-effective procedure for noise abatement should take into account the different noise impacts around different airports.

The tax also would vary with the effective perceived noise level (EPNL) per operation. The average tax per EPNL decibel was calculated by dividing the estimate of $146 million a year in property loss by the average number of NEF decibels above thirty that the average person living within the thirty NEF contour experiences.[23] The calculations result in an average tax rate of $2.47 per EPNL per operation.[24] Although the amount appears to be small, the numbers add up quickly. On average, a Boeing 707 would be taxed $54.34 per landing and $44.46 per takeoff. If the aircraft were retrofitted with

---

[20] This is because the NEF formula weighs nighttime operations about twelve times more heavily than daytime operations.

[21] See Department of Transportation, *Aircraft Noise Pollution Forecast*, vol. 1.

[22] If the difference in the average property values around the two cities were taken into account, the difference in the noise taxes would be even greater.

[23] These calculations are shown in the appendix.

[24] This tax rate would become effective (because of the NEF formula) at approximately 95 decibels, depending on the intensity of the use of the given airport. This study has calculated average decibel tax rates. In practice, however, the tax rate per decibel would increase exponentially because the area of the NEF noise contours increases exponentially with NEF levels.

quiet nacelles (shelters for the engines), the tax would be only $17.78 for each takeoff or landing.[25] The sum of the takeoff and landing differences of $63.24 amounts to about $63,000 a year at 1,000 departures a year. According to EPA, the retrofit of a 707 would cost about $1.12 million (1972 dollars).[26] The airlines would thus have to be able to borrow capital at 5.6 percent interest for the tax incentive to make it profitable to retrofit.[27] Hence, the cost of borrowing would be prohibitive at either the current interest rate or the 10 percent interest rate assumed here for purposes of illustration.

Thus, although the proposed tax system might not create significant incentives to retrofit or refan aircraft, it would create incentives to reduce the use of aircraft that do not meet FAR 36 standards and increase the use of the quieter and larger wide-bodied aircraft. On the basis of the same calculation technique employed above, the DC-10-40 would be expected to generate $39,000 in noise taxes per year, or a net savings of $49,000 of noise taxes compared with a 707 that was not retrofitted.[28] If, in addition, the rule of thumb that one DC-10 substitutes for two 707s is used, then the total savings in noise tax from shifting to the DC-10 would be $158,000 a year. These tax savings, along with the other variables entering a decision to replace aircraft, would be considered by management, thus producing many cost-effective and gradual improvements in noise abatement.

The exact magnitude of the total NEF reduction throughout the country cannot be calculated because of the many possible methods of noise abatement. The advantage of this system is that a given unit of noise abatement would be achieved at minimum costs. The actual tax rates chosen would not affect this characteristic of cost-effectiveness. The rate chosen in this study, however, is an estimate

---

[25] The figures are calculated by multiplying $2.47 times the EPA estimated EPN decibel levels above 95 for retrofit and without retrofit. See Environmental Protection Agency, *Project Report*, p. 11-6.

[26] Ibid., p. 11-7. The EPA estimate was in terms of 1973 dollars. That figure has been discounted to 1972 by 7 percent to make their estimate compatible with this study's estimates.

[27] This finding is consistent with the cost-benefit analysis of the retrofit proposal that was cited above. The 5.6 percent rate assumes no amortization in order to allow direct comparison with the $146 million estimate for the losses in property taxes given above.

[28] With the same assumptions as above, the Concorde would be expected to generate more than $106,000 a year in noise-tax revenues compared with the $63,000 and $39,000 estimates for the 707 and DC-10, respectively. These estimates are based on a constant-decibel tax rate. Use of the more proper increasing marginal tax rate would increase these relative cost differences.

of the optimal rate—that is, the rate at which marginal social costs equal marginal social benefits.[29] If society collectively places a larger value on noise abatement than the people living around airports evidently do, a higher tax rate could be chosen.

Distribution of the Tax Revenue

Two other areas should be considered in the study: distribution of the tax revenues collected and implementation of the tax-incentive approach. Although the overall advantage of the tax-incentive approach may not turn upon these issues, they would be of significant practical concern in considering such a system. In both these areas a variety of approaches is possible, and each should be examined by further study.

The first issue is what to do with the tax revenues. One set of possibilities would be to put them with general revenues or to return them to the airlines on an allocation basis other than noise generation. It could even be required that these funds be earmarked for retrofitting aircraft. These possibilities would be relatively easy to implement, but would do little or nothing to recompense those who are harmed by the continuing aircraft noise pollution.

An alternative approach would be to compensate directly those who have been harmed by aircraft noise on a yearly basis as taxes are collected. Again, there are several possibilities. Payments could be provided to people now living in high-noise areas regardless of when they purchased their homes. Although this approach would be relatively simple to administer, it would result in some windfall profits to people who purchased their property knowing of the noise problem. A second approach would be to compensate the people who have suffered losses in their property value. These people purchased their property before the noise was present and had the value of their property diminished by the noise. This latter approach, however, would require tracking people who have moved away and therefore would be much more difficult to implement.[30] Under either approach, the issue of whether recipients would still have the right to sue for damages caused by noise pollution would have to be addressed. One advantage of the direct-compensation approach (whether

---

[29] In actual practice, there would be not one rate but a rate schedule that increases with the number of decibels generated.

[30] After only five years, up to half the residents of a neighborhood may have moved out. See John Goodman, "Local Mobility and Family Housing Adjustment" (unpublished paper, University of Michigan).

to present dwellers or to former and present dwellers who suffered a loss) is that it appears to promote a more equal distribution of income. Surveys of air travelers show that air travelers (who would be expected to pay higher fares) have higher incomes than the general population, and therefore higher incomes than most people who live or have lived near airports.

A second issue to be studied is what level of government should decide upon and implement the aircraft noise tax. The alternatives are the federal government (presumably FAA, if authorized by the Congress) or local governmental authorities. Giving responsibility to the federal government would better assure uniformity of application and would avoid the possibility that local governments might charge either zero taxes or taxes that were too high and damaging to aviation. On the other hand, the issue of who received compensation appears more resolvable at the local level and would be expected to lead to an "optimal demand for noise pollution." Implicit in this idea is that the attainment of a zero level of pollution would cost society more than society would benefit. At zero noise pollution there would be no tax collections and therefore no compensation. Under a regulatory scheme or tax system without transfers to the injured party, the injured party has an incentive to demand that something be done about pollution beyond the optimum and up to the point of zero pollution. Under a transfer scheme, the demand would end when the marginal social benefits of further pollution abatement equaled the marginal social cost of achieving that abatement. Presumably, families would choose through the political process between further noise abatement and reduced compensation. If, however, the optimal tax rate can be calculated (as has been attempted above), the compensation mechanism of the local government would not be required on efficiency grounds, although on equity grounds it may still be desirable.

The Recommendation

The issues of whether to establish a tax-incentive approach to aircraft noise and the general level of revenues to be collected through this approach have been discussed. The advantages that would be expected to result from adopting such a system have been outlined. Those advantages should be carefully examined, and it should be determined whether there are any substantial countervailing disadvantages. It would appear, however, that a tax-incentive approach is clearly superior to the current regulatory approach.

The advantages of the effluent-charge approach have long been argued by a wide range of experts both inside and outside government. In other areas, administrative problems have evidently slowed up their acceptance. In this area, however, the small number of emission sources and new techniques of measurement make the tax-incentive approach a promising alternative and an excellent test case of the feasibility of implementing effluent charges.

Appendix: Technical Calculations

Calculation of Total Cost of Aircraft Noise. The required data for calculating the total cost of aircraft noise are the EPA estimates of cumulative noise exposure for 1972 from Tables 10–16 of the Environmental Protection Agency's *Project Report*. These numbers were divided by three to determine the number of families living within the noise contours. The number of NEF decibels to which each family was subject was estimated by a straight-line extrapolation between NEF interval classes. The average 1972 metropolitan property value per family and the depreciation rate per NEF was then multiplied by the cumulative noise exposure estimate as in the following formula:

$$c = P \cdot d \cdot 5 \cdot \sum_{i=1}^{n} [N_{i+1} + \tfrac{1}{2}(N_i - N_{i+1})],$$

where c = the estimated property loss plus $1.457 billion
P = the 1972 metropolitan property value estimate of $20,100 per property (including rental units), calculated by taking a weighted average of 1970 census estimates of property values and capitalized rents and inflating by 6 percent per year.[31]
d = the 0.5 percent depreciation rate per NEF
5 = the number of NEF decibels per interval
N = the number of families per NEF interval i
i = 1, 2, 3, 4, = 30 NEF, 35 NEF, 40 NEF, 45 NEF and over
N_1 = 2.5 million families
N_2 = 1.1 million families
N_3 = 0.5 million families
N_4 = 0.1 million families.

[31] Council on Wage and Price Stability, "Comments of the Council on Wage and Price Stability Regarding Proposed Aircraft Noise Retrofit Requirements," pp. 11–12.

Calculation of the NEF Exposure. The average NEF exposure above 30 NEF for the average family exposed above 30 NEF was calculated using the formula:

$$A = \frac{\sum\limits_{i=1}^{n} (N_1 - N_{i+1})}{N_1} = 5.9 \text{ NEF decibels}$$

where $A =$ the average NEF level, and the other symbols are the same as above.

The noise-charge approach has not as yet been adopted by the FAA or any major domestic airports, although the FAA is continuing to fund research on the approach. The agency has also initiated further econometric studies designed to estimate the effect on property value of noise around airports. On April 15, 1977, the Council on Wage and Price Stability submitted formal testimony to the FAA urging that the noise-charge approach be considered.[32] The FAA, however, has continued its basic regulatory strategy for controlling airport noise. It has mandated that existing aircraft meet the FAR 36 requirements by 1985 and that new generation aircraft meet even tighter standards.

---

[32] Council on Wage and Price Stability, "Noise Charge Approach to Reducing Airport Noise," CWPS-240 (April 15, 1977).

12

Domestic Sugar Producers and International Competition

Thomas M. Lenard

The United States maintained an income support program for sugar producers from the 1930s through 1974. This program restricted the amount of sugar individual countries could export to the United States. The program was allowed to expire after sugar prices rose to record levels in 1974. The world price of raw sugar, which for the most part had been below five cents a pound before 1972, reached about sixty cents a pound during 1974. By the end of 1976, most of this price rise had been eliminated, and there were renewed pressures for government support and protection from imports.

The International Trade Commission (ITC), at the request of the Senate Finance Committee and with the endorsement of the President, has opened an investigation under section 201 of the Trade Act of 1974 relating to sugar.[1] At the conclusion of the investigation, the ITC is required to make an affirmative or negative finding on the question of whether domestic producers have been injured by imports. If that decision is in the affirmative, the ITC then recommends to the President one of the following remedies: adjustment assistance, tariff increases, tariff rate quotas (whereby the tariff is adjusted to the volume of imports), or import quotas. Upon receipt of the ITC's recommendations, the President has sixty days to make a decision.

This report supports the view that any measure which would

This chapter is edited from "Investigation No. TA-201-16: Sugar," Comments of the Council on Wage and Price Stability before the U.S. International Trade Commission, December 20, 1976.

[1] 88 Stat. 1978. In addition to his support of the sugar investigation, on September 21, 1976, the President announced a tripling of the duty on imported sugar (from 0.625 cents to 1.875 cents a pound) as an interim measure. These actions were taken as temporary steps toward a permanent action.

artificially reduce imports—tariffs, quotas, or some combination—would impose costs on society that are greater than any benefits derived. The costs induced by artificial barriers to trade generally fall on consumers in the form of higher prices, and these costs exceed the benefits that might be enjoyed by producers in the form of increased profits. Consequently, a tariff or quota action is inflationary. Put differently, the costs of barriers to trade exceed the benefits. Because of these inflationary effects, the commission should consider this analysis of the impact on prices of the requested quotas, and include the results of the analysis in its report to the President. A report of such data is clearly envisioned by the Trade Act of 1974, which directs the President to make his final decision on the basis of factors that include "the effect of import relief on consumers (including the price and availability of the imported article and the like or directly competitive article produced in the United States) and on competition in the domestic markets for such articles."[2] If, on the basis of such factors, the President finds that import relief would not be "in the national economic interest of the United States," the President is authorized to deny import relief.[3] Indeed, the act expressly authorizes the President to request such information where the commission has not submitted it to him.[4]

Economic Effects of Trade Barriers

As indicated above, increasing the import duty on sugar or adopting a quota to restrict sugar imports would be inflationary. Although domestic producers would receive higher profits because of the duty or the quota, and although the government would collect some additional customs revenue in the case of a tariff increase, consumers would pay higher prices for sugar. Most important, the total amount by which producers' profits plus customs duties (or any other benefits) would increase would be less than the increase in costs to consumers. The difference between these amounts would be a loss to society as a whole and would add to inflation. Therefore, the com-

---

[2] See section 202(c)(4) of the Trade Act, 19 U.S.C., section 2252(c)(4).

[3] Ibid., section 2252(b)(1).

[4] See ibid., section 2252(d), which provides that the President may, within fifteen days after the date on which he receives an affirmative finding of the commission under section 201(b) with respect to an industry, request additional information from the commission. The commission shall, as soon as practicable but in no event more than thirty days after the date on which it receives the President's request, furnish additional information about that industry in a supplemental report.

mission, if it arrives at a finding of injury, should recommend adjustment assistance rather than quotas or duties in order to minimize the social cost of its actions.

Two subsidiary points should be made. First, to some extent, the recent fall in the profits of domestic sugar producers is the result of increased competition from high-fructose corn syrup, a sugar substitute. This competition indicates that quotas or tariffs may not be particularly helpful to domestic sugar producers, since an increase in the price of sugar would serve as an even greater incentive for increased production of high-fructose corn syrup.

Second, the concern for sugar prices expressed here goes back to the autumn of 1974, when retail sugar prices rose to 79 cents a pound. At that time, the Council on Wage and Price Stability held hearings on sugar prices and issued a special report of the findings. The report noted the important function of increased profits to growers and processors during a time of relative shortage in the supply of sugar and pointed out that, for the free market economy to provide sugar at reasonable prices in the amounts desired by consumers, producers must be willing to compete during all market conditions, not merely during times of high profits.

An Increase in the Duty on Imported Sugar

Increasing the duty on imported sugar has the effect of raising the price consumers pay and the price domestic producers receive. This price increase in turn causes domestic sugar consumption (that is, consumption of imported sugar plus domestically produced sugar) to decrease, increases domestic sugar production, and leads to a decrease of imports. In addition, an increase in the duty has the effect of transferring income from consumers to producers and the government. This mechanism creates an inefficient use of economic resources, which generates a social cost for which there is no offsetting social gain.

A graphical illustration of the effect of an increase in the duty on sugar is presented in Figure 12–1 in the appendix to this chapter. The sources of inefficiency lie in the fact that an increase in the duty decreases domestic consumption and increases domestic production. The decrease in consumption represents a loss in consumer surplus since the value of the additional sugar to consumers exceeds its cost of production.[5] The substitution of domestic for imported sugar

---

[5] Consumer surplus denotes the value consumers attach to sugar in excess of the price they pay.

represents an additional cost caused by inefficient resource use since the additional sugar is produced domestically at a cost higher than the world cost of production. This additional cost is passed on to consumers. To summarize, increasing the duty on imported sugar involves a welfare loss both in consumer surplus and because of inefficient production.

Raising the price of sugar by increasing the duty also increases returns to domestic producers above the cost of the resources needed to produce the additional sugar. This increase in profits is a pure transfer from consumers to producers that represents no net cost to society. In addition, increasing the duty generates additional revenues received by the government.[6]

Thus, increasing the duty on imported sugar would yield benefits to domestic sugar producers and would increase government receipts. On the other hand, the costs would be higher prices for consumers who stay in the market and forgone purchases for consumers who leave the market because of the higher price. The question is: Do the benefits exceed the costs? And the answer is, unambiguously, no; the costs always exceed the benefits.

To estimate the magnitude of these costs and benefits, the effects of tripling the duty on sugar have been calculated on the assumption that initially sugar sells for $12 a hundredweight.[7] The price of sugar has been fluctuating near this level. In addition, it is assumed that at present domestic production is 6.6 million tons a year, imports are 4.4 million tons a year, and domestic consumption is 11.0 million tons a year.[8]

Finally, estimates of the elasticities of supply and demand (providing measures of the sensitivity of supply and demand to changes in price) are needed to estimate the effects of an increase in the duty. Initially, it is assumed that the elasticity of domestic supply for sugar is 0.4 and the elasticity of demand is —0.05.[9] In addition, it is as-

---

[6] Whether this represents a net cost or a net gain depends on the productivity of government expenditures. This paper assumes that the government spends its money as well as (and no better than) consumers would and that, consequently, there is no net social cost or benefit involved here.

[7] For computational convenience, it is assumed that the duty is increased from $0.60 to $1.80 a hundredweight. This simplification does not affect the conclusion with respect to the inflationary effects of tariffs and quotas.

[8] These figures approximate the current situation according to data from the U.S. Department of Agriculture.

[9] For elasticity of domestic supply, see E.V. Jesse, "U.S. Beet Sugar Supply Response" (unpublished manuscript, U.S. Department of Agriculture, Economic Research Service, 1976). Because no elasticity estimate for cane sugar is available, this estimate for domestic supply in general is being used. It should be

TABLE 12–1

ANNUAL EFFECTS OF TRIPLING THE DUTY ON IMPORTED SUGAR:
TWO SCENARIOS
(millions of dollars)

Elasticity of Supply = 0.4; Elasticity of Demand = −0.05[a]

Benefits	
Increased returns to domestic producers	161.6
Increase in government receipts	94.1
Total benefits	255.7
Total cost to consumers	263.3
Net cost (total cost minus total benefits)	7.7

Elasticity of Supply = 1.0; Elasticity of Demand = −1.0[b]

Benefits	
Increased returns to domestic producers	166.3
Increase in government receipts	42.2
Total benefits	208.6
Total cost to consumers	250.8
Net cost (total cost minus total benefits)	42.2

[a] Given these assumptions, domestic consumption will decrease by 0.06 million tons, domestic production will increase by 0.26 million tons, and imports will decrease by 0.32 million tons annually.

[b] Given these assumptions, domestic consumption will decline by 1.1 million tons, domestic production will rise by 0.66 million tons, and imports will decline by 1.76 million tons annually.

sumed that foreign supply is perfectly elastic since the United States takes a relatively small portion of the world supply (which is approximately 90 million tons annually).[10]

The elasticity estimates used in this example are for the short run, and consequently the estimated effects are relevant for that time period. The data summarized in the upper half of Table 12–1 indicate a total cost to consumers of more than $260 million a year.[11] Since $160 million of this is a transfer to producers and $94 million

noted that the cane supply elasticity is generally considered to be smaller than the beet elasticity. For elasticity of demand, see G. Gemmill, "The World Sugar Economy: An Econometric Analysis of Production and Policies" (Ph.D. dissertation, Michigan State University, January 1976).

[10] U.S. Department of Agriculture. No estimate of the world elasticity of supply is available, and some may challenge the assumption used here. If the world supply is not perfectly elastic (as may be the case in the short run), the price to domestic consumers will not rise by the full amount of the tariff and the costs to consumers will be smaller. The conclusion—that costs exceed benefits—is not affected, however.

[11] The derivation of these figures is carried out in the appendix for this set of elasticities.

is a transfer to the government, the remaining net cost is more than $7 million. This $7 million is the associated deadweight loss of the trade restrictions, a waste of economic resources. Any such reduction in the aggregate supply of goods and services has inflationary effects on the economy.

The elasticities used in this example are probably not valid in the long run. As a general rule, elasticities will increase as producers and consumers have a longer time in which to adjust to their behavior. Especially on the demand side, when the recent inroads of high-fructose corn syrup into the market are considered, elasticity can be expected to increase. Since no estimates of long-run elasticities are available, to gain some perspective on the longer run the effects of a duty increase have been recomputed assuming that the elasticities of demand and supply are each unity (negative and positive, respectively). The results are summarized in the lower half of Table 12–1. While the total cost to consumers is smaller than in the previous case, the amount of the deadweight loss—more than $40 million a year— is substantially larger. This is the most important element of cost since it represents a waste of economic resources.

Effects of Restrictive Quotas

An alternative to increasing tariffs is establishing quotas. Of course, a tariff has the restrictive effects of a quota. For example, a tariff that decreases imports by 1.75 million tons annually is equivalent to a yearly quota that restricts imports by that amount.

Other effects associated with a quota should also be considered. At present, a quota of 7 million tons a year is in effect; since the current level of imports is 4.4 million tons a year, this has no effect. But, for the purposes of this example, the effects of instituting a binding quota of 4 million tons a year can be considered.

The effects of such a quota are described in the appendix and are summarized in Table 12–2 for both sets of elasticities used previously. In this example, the sources of costs and their interpretation are similar to the case of a tariff increase. In the case of a quota, however, there may be a substantial transfer to foreign producers as a result of the implicit price rise necessary to decrease imports enough to comply with the quota.[12] This transfer is, in some sense, comparable to the transfer to the U.S. government that would occur in the case of a tariff increase. Also, government receipts will fall (for any level of tariff) as imports fall.

---

[12] As imports are reduced, the domestic price must rise to clear the market.

TABLE 12–2

ANNUAL EFFECTS OF A QUOTA OF FOUR MILLION TONS
(millions of dollars)

Elasticity of Supply = 0.4; Elasticity of Demand = −0.05[a]

Benefits	
Increased returns to domestic producers	203.0
Transfers to foreign producers	120.0
Total benefits	323.0
Costs	
Decline in U.S. government receipts[b]	4.8
Cost to consumers	329.0
Total cost	333.8
Net cost (total cost minus total benefits)	10.8

Elasticity of Supply = 1.0; Elasticity of Demand = −1.0[c]

Benefits	
Increased returns to domestic producers	36.0
Transfers to foreign producers	21.6
Total benefits	57.6
Costs	
Decline in U.S. government receipts[b]	4.8
Cost to consumers	58.7
Total cost	63.5
Net cost (total cost minus total benefits)	5.9

[a] Given these assumptions, the price of sugar will rise by $1.50 per hundredweight (cwt.), domestic consumption will decline by 0.07 million tons, and domestic production will rise by 0.33 million tons annually.

[b] Assuming a duty of $0.60 per cwt.

[c] Given these assumptions, the price of sugar will rise by $0.27 per cwt., domestic consumption will decline by 0.25 million tons, and domestic production will rise by 0.15 million tons annually.

Though the computed deadweight loss in social welfare is relatively small, the total cost to consumers and the total transfer to domestic producers are large, especially when the elasticities are small. In contrast to an increase in the duty, with a quota the deadweight loss and transfers to producers decline with increased elasticities (as would be the case in the long run) because the price rise implied by the quota declines. Demand could also be expected to increase over time, however, and this would tend to increase the social cost of the quota.

Effects of Sugar Substitutes

The above illustrations, which provide an indication of the magnitude of the costs of adopting tariffs or quotas, assume that the domestic

167

sugar market can, in fact, be protected. This possibility of protection should be examined in light of recent developments in the high-fructose corn syrup industry. High-fructose corn syrup is a close substitute for sugar in many manufacturing uses and, depending on corn prices, provides stiff competition for sugar. As the price of sugar increases, more consumers shift to the substitute; this is one reason the demand for sugar may be much more elastic in the long run. Therefore, over the long run, a tariff or a quota may not result in a substantial increase in domestic sugar production.

If protective action—in the form of increased tariffs or decreased quotas—for sugar is taken, the effect may be to aid the high-fructose corn syrup industry and provide little assistance for sugar producers. Since present indications are that high-fructose corn syrup is very competitive with and substitutable for sugar, it may in fact be difficult to provide any meaningful protection for the domestic sugar industry.[13] Therefore, the ITC should, as a part of its investigation, determine the effects of the recent developments in the high-fructose corn syrup industry.

Conclusion

Though the examples presented here are mainly for illustrative purposes, they do provide an indication of the magnitude of the costs that would be imposed on consumers and on society by tariffs or quotas applied to imported sugar. As indicated, these costs are significant. Furthermore, the imposition of tariffs or quotas is always inefficient since costs always exceed benefits. Therefore, if the ITC finds that injury has occurred, adjustment assistance would be the form of redress with the least probability for inflationary effects.

Appendix

Effects of Tripling the Duty. In this appendix, the effects of tripling the duty on imported sugar from $0.60 per hundredweight (cwt.) to $1.80 per cwt. are analyzed. It is assumed that initially sugar was selling for $12.00 per cwt. (including the $0.60 duty).

It is assumed that domestic production is 6.6 million tons (132

---

[13] This will depend on how quickly high-fructose corn syrup is adopted in the future. But the indications are that it will be very competitive. For example, one estimate suggests that high-fructose corn syrup can be produced for nine cents a pound (excluding marketing costs) when corn is $2.70 a bushel. See George Tsao, "High Fructose Syrups," mimeographed (Lafayette, Indiana: Purdue University, 1976).

million cwt.) a year, that domestic consumption is 11 million tons (220 million cwt.), and that imports are 4.4 million tons (88 million cwt.). These figures approximate the current situation.

For the purposes of this illustration, it is assumed that: $E_d = -0.05$ (where E_d = elasticity of domestic demand) and $E_s = 0.4$ (where E_s = elasticity of domestic supply). The foreign supply curve is assumed to be perfectly elastic.

Given these assumptions, the effect of tripling the duty is summarized in Figure 12–1. The effects of this action (where D = domestic demand and S^d = domestic supply) are: [14]

- Percentage change in price = $t = 0.1$.

- Change in domestic consumption = $E_d D t = -1.1$ million cwt. (-0.55 million tons).

- Change in domestic production = $E_s S^d t = 5.28$ million cwt. (0.264 million tons).

- Change in imports = -6.38 million cwt. (-0.319 million tons).

Effects of a Quota of 4 Million Tons. At present, a quota of 7 million tons is in effect. Given the present level of imports (approximately 4.4 million tons), this quota has no effect. It is useful, however, to examine the effects of instituting a binding quota of 4 million tons.

As above, it is assumed that $E_d = -0.05$ and $E_s = 0.4$. The change in imports = -8.0 million cwt. (or 0.4 million tons) = $E_d D t - E_s S^d t$. The percentage change in price (t) = 0.125. That is, the price will rise by \$1.50 or 12.5 percent. This implies that domestic consumption will decline by 1.4 million cwt. (0.07 million tons) and domestic production will rise by 6.6 million cwt. (0.33 million tons). These results are summarized in Figure 12–2.

On March 17, 1977, the ITC reported to President Carter that the domestic sugar industry was being threatened with serious injury by increased imports and recommended that quota restraints be imposed on imports to relieve the threat. The commission was evenly divided on whether the annual quota should be set at 4.275 million tons or 4.4 million tons.

A month and a half later, on May 4, the President announced that he would not provide import relief either through quotas or

---

[14] In these calculations, the initial levels of domestic production and consumption are used.

FIGURE 12–1

EFFECTS OF AN INCREASED SUGAR TARIFF
(not drawn to scale)

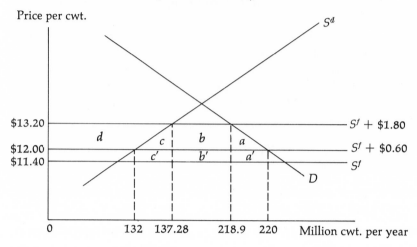

where D = domestic demand
S^d = domestic supply
S^f = foreign supply (before increase in duty)

$a + a'$ = loss in consumer surplus = $1.32 million.
$c + c'$ = loss due to inefficient production = $6.336 million.
$a + a' + c + c'$ = total welfare loss = $7.656 million.
d = increased rents to domestic producers = $161.568 million.
$b - a' - c'$ = change in U.S. government receipts = $94.116 million.
$a + b + c + d$ = total incremental cost to consumers = $263.34 million.

Note that a portion of the transfer under the $0.60 duty turns into a welfare loss when the duty is increased. This loss is given by $a' + c'$.

through tariffs. Instead, he requested the secretary of agriculture to institute an income support program offering payments of up to 2 cents a pound to sugar producers whenever the market price fell below 13.5 cents a pound, pending the negotiation of an International Sugar Agreement (ISA). The payment program was announced by the secretary on September 15, 1977, but later was superseded by a sugar loan program, required by the Food and Agriculture Act of 1977, which supported the price of raw sugar at 13.5 cents a pound.

To prevent imports from interfering with the support program, the President, in November 1977, raised import duties and fees by

FIGURE 12–2

EFFECTS OF A BINDING SUGAR QUOTA
(not drawn to scale)

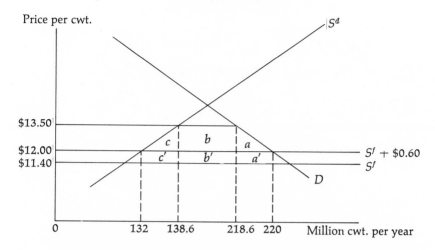

$a + a' = \$1.89$ million, $c + c' = \$8.91$ million.
$a + a' + c + c' =$ total welfare loss $= \$10.8$ million.
$d =$ increased rents to domestic producers $= \$202.95$ million.
$b =$ increased rents to foreign producers $= \$120$ million.
$a' + c' =$ loss in U.S. government receipts $= \$4.80$ million.
$a + b + c + d =$ total cost to consumers $= \$328.95$ million.

the amount necessary to reach the support level. He also requested that the ITC investigate whether imports were materially interfering with the support program. On April 17, 1978, the ITC reported to the President that imports were interfering and recommended additional import fees and lower quotas.

At this writing, an ISA has been negotiated and is awaiting approval by the Senate. As negotiated, the ISA establishes a mechanism to keep world sugar prices between 11 and 21 cents a pound.

On January 1, 1979, President Carter increased the import fee on sugar to bring the domestic price to 15 cents per pound.